One Beat More

One Beat More

Existentialism and the
Gift of Mortality

Kevin Aho

polity

The right of Kevin Aho to be identified as Author of this Work has been asserted in accordance with the UK Copyright, Designs and Patents Act 1988.

First published in 2022 by Polity Press

Polity Press
65 Bridge Street
Cambridge CB2 1UR, UK

Polity Press
101 Station Landing
Suite 300
Medford, MA 02155, USA

ISBN-13: 978-1-5095-4689-3
ISBN-13: 978-1-5095-4690-9(pb)

A catalogue record for this book is available from the British Library.

Library of Congress Control Number: 2021945096

Typeset in 11 on 12pt Sabon
by Cheshire Typesetting Ltd, Cuddington, Cheshire
Printed and bound in the UK by TJ Books Limited

The publisher has used its best endeavours to ensure that the URLs for external websites referred to in this book are correct and active at the time of going to press. However, the publisher has no responsibility for the websites and can make no guarantee that a site will remain live or that the content is or will remain appropriate.

Every effort has been made to trace all copyright holders, but if any have been overlooked the publisher will be pleased to include any necessary credits in any subsequent reprint or edition.

For further information on Polity, visit our website: politybooks.com

Die while you're alive, and be absolutely dead. Then do
whatever you want: it's all good.

Shidō Bunan (1603–1676)

Contents

Acknowledgments

First off, I want to express my gratitude to the doctors and nurses who saved my life and took care of me as I recovered at the Gulf Coast Medical Center in Fort Myers, Florida. I am singularly grateful to my cardiologist, Nemalan Selveraj, and to my primary care physician, Shaila Hegde, both of whom embody a rare dedication to the healing arts and an extraordinary capacity for empathy. I also want to pay tribute to the amazing group of nurses at the Institute for Hermeneutic Phenomenology at the University of Buffalo's College of Nursing. Among this group, I am especially thankful to Annie Vandermause and Suzanne Dickerson, whose friendship and support have been invaluable to me. And there are a number of philosophers, medical humanists, and scholars whose work inspired me and helped guide this project along, including Havi Carel, Arthur Frank, Joseph Davis, Gordon Marino, Drew Leder, Nicole Piemonte, Richard Polt, Fredrik Svenaeus, and the late Charles Guignon.

The initial ideas for this book came about in the weeks and months that followed my heart attack in

Acknowledgments

December 2017. In an effort to make sense of my collapsing world, I worked on a couple of essays. The first was a short narrative of the experience, "Notes from a Heart Attack: A Phenomenology of an Altered Body," later published in the collection *Phenomenology of the Broken Body*, edited by Espen Dahl, Cassandra Falke, and Thor Eirik Eriksen (London: Routledge, 2019). At around the same time, the sociologist Joseph Davis reached out and invited me to a conference on the ethics of aging held at the Institute for Advanced Studies in Culture at the University of Virginia. I was too anxious and weak to travel at the time but managed to write a paper for the event: "The Contraction of Time and Existential Awakening: A Phenomenology of Authentic Aging." The conference papers were published in the collection *The Evening of Life: The Challenges of Aging and Dying Well* (Notre Dame, IN: University of Notre Dame Press, 2020). I am grateful to the editors of these two collections and to Routledge and the University of Notre Dame Press for permission to reprint portions of these chapters.

The excellent editorial team at Polity has once again exceeded all my expectations. I am deeply grateful to my commissioning editor, Pascal Porcheron, who was an early champion of the project and encouraged me to make the book more personal, in an effort to disclose more of my own emotional and philosophical struggles. He went through the entire manuscript line by line, offering valuable feedback and commentary throughout. And Manuela Tecusan's masterful copyediting greatly improved the writing and corrected countless syntactical blunders. I am also grateful to two anonymous reviewers for their critical feedback and recommendations.

Acknowledgments

I also want to thank my loving partner, Jane Kayser, who was with me for the entire journey and offered unwavering support and encouragement as she listened to me read aloud from early chapters of the book. But, more than anyone, I am thankful to my parents, Jim and Margaret Aho. In the autumn of their own lives, they have taught me what it means to face up to mortality and to live with a sense of awe, gratitude, and joy. This book is dedicated to them.

Introduction

To Learn How to Die

It was a beautiful, sun-dappled December morning in south Florida. The sky was blue, the humidity low, and there was not a breath of wind as I began my bike ride through leafy neighborhoods in Naples, Bonita Springs, and Fort Myers. Three-and-a-half hours and sixty miles later, I was pedaling over the Estero Bridge toward my house and was suddenly overcome with nausea and lightheadedness. I squeezed the brakes, threw my bike to the ground, and vomited all over the street. Confused and thinking I had food poisoning or simply overdid it on the ride, I slowly rode back home. Then the chest pain came as a dull, persistent ache. I called my girlfriend, telling her that I was having some trouble. She said it sounded like I was having a heart attack. I dismissed it. "No, I'm just hungry and dehydrated and need to take a shower." She raced to my house and convinced me to go to the hospital as the dizziness deepened. After a quick ECG in the emergency room, I was ushered into a suite of scurrying doctors and nurses who were already preparing the surgery. All I heard above the din was, "Massive heart

1

attack ... Widowmaker ... LAD blocked ... LAD blocked!"

A week after my heart attack was Christmas Day, and I was deeply shaken as I began to take the first tentative steps back into my life. I wanted to begin the day with a slow stroll around the block, but only got to the end of the driveway. My right calf felt tight and achy and my toes were numb. I came back to the house with a grim face: "Something's wrong." My girlfriend rushed me back to the hospital, where I received an ultrasound on my leg and, sure enough, a dangerous blood clot was found in my femoral artery. There were multiple days of treatment with a vascular surgeon, angiograms to examine the clot, and various tubes inserted through my left groin down to my right calf. (The right groin couldn't be used, as this was the side that they had gone up in order to place the stent in my heart.) The surgeon was unable to remove the clot, so he opted for an aggressive intravenous clot buster treatment combined with high doses of blood thinners. I was unable to eat or stand for three days. Every hour, nurses would measure the size of my calf to see if blood was flowing, and each hour I was gripped by terror that the clot was getting larger or the pulse in my right foot was getting weaker. Each night was a din of buzzers, beeps, blood tests, and vital sign checks. I slept in fits and starts.

I was finally released from intensive care after the clot buster medication had done its work, and I was able to move to my own hospital room for observation. The diagnosis was that a clot in my heart had been discharged during the heart attack, and that I would need to be on a battery of blood thinners to prevent future clots from forming. On the second night of observation, an alarm and flashing red light erupted from the heart monitor that hung on the wall; it signalled a thirty-second burst of ventricular tachycardia. The next morning my cardiologist warned me that I had experienced a potentially deadly arrhythmia, which made me vulnerable to what he called "sudden cardiac death." The solution was to wear a portable heart defibrillator (or "life vest") for the next few months, as the clot dissolved, and then decide whether or not to implant an electronic defibrillator in my chest.

The combined effect of these events left me shattered. I was only forty-eight years old but suddenly felt old and frail. Ordinary tasks such as walking up the stairs or getting out of the car left me exhausted and out of breath. My future, once open and expansive with possibilities, had collapsed. And the interpretation I had of myself as a healthy and energetic college professor fell to pieces. I felt trapped in a meaningless present, left to the moment-to-moment rituals of taking medication, checking my blood pressure and pulse, and arranging the next doctor visit. I was suddenly forced to confront the existential questions I had spent so many years teaching and writing about, "Who am I?" and "What is the meaning of my life?" Indeed, the ideas of existentialism, that distinctive brand of European philosophy that exploded on the scene in mid-twentieth-century France, became an obsession for me as I convalesced at home, frightened and vulnerable. Its focus on the flesh-and-blood experiences of the individual, its emphasis on being authentic and honest about our condition, and its engagement with the ultimate questions of human existence, of the meaning of life and death, were more pressing and vital to me than ever. And I began to see

3

the ideas of existentialism being played out in real life in my biweekly sessions of cardiac rehab.

Here nurses would put a group of heart attack survivors on treadmills and rowing machines and gently encourage us to exercise for thirty minutes while carefully monitoring our heart rate and blood pressure. I was at least twenty years younger than anyone else in the room, and over the course of these sessions I began to talk with and learn from my elders. What struck me initially was how differently they seemed to interpret the experience of their failing bodies. Whereas I was gripped by dread and was hypervigilant about every skipped heartbeat and flashing pain in my chest, they appeared far less shaken. They spoke of the importance of not worrying about things you can't control, about letting go and taking pleasure in little things. There was an elderly woman, Beverly, who appeared to sense my distress. She sat next to me at the end of one of my final sessions and said: "As you get older, Kevin, these kinds of things just get easier to accept. I can't explain it." Her words were strange, but they comforted me. Here, in a cardiac rehab clinic, I seemed to be surrounded by folks who already embodied a kind of existential wisdom. Whereas I was riddled with despair, they seemed clearsighted about their condition, talked openly about their physical pain and losses, and appeared calmer and more sanguine in the face of mortality. Their weakened and frail bodies reminded me of death, but their attitudes seemed freer to me, more life-affirming. I began to think that maybe there was something about growing old that can make us more honest and accepting about who we are, something that can help us place our everyday worries in a proper perspective, and that maybe we become more like the existentialists as we get older.

As I began to do more research on the wisdom that comes with growing old, this suspicion grew stronger. A key moment occurred when I happened across a remarkable series of articles in the *New York Times* by journalist John Leland, who had spent a year closely documenting the lives of six ordinary New Yorkers from diverse backgrounds who were all members of the "oldest old," that is, eighty-five years and up. Leland's series was later published as a book, titled *Happiness Is a Choice You Make: Lessons from a Year among the Oldest Old*, and in its pages the reader is introduced to elders who struggled with painful illnesses, loss, and bodily diminishment but who nonetheless lived with a marked sense of purpose and joy. Like Beverly, who consoled me at cardiac rehab, these elders weren't dwelling on their losses or missed opportunities, nor were they overly anxious about the nearness of their own death. Indeed, they all seemed to shatter the ageist stereotypes I had grown accustomed to. Fred, for example, an eighty-seven-year-old African American and World War II veteran with debilitating heart disease whom Leland became especially fond of in the course of his research, accepted his bodily limitations and the proximity of death with a kind of ease and lightness. He embraced his age and savored each moment as it came with a clear knowledge that his time was short. Leland was struck by how Fred didn't look backward with regret or forward with anticipation. He existed in the present. When he asked when the happiest period of his life was, Fred replied without hesitation, "Right now."[1] Fred was what the German philosopher Friedrich

Nietzsche would have called a "yes-sayer," someone who embraces and affirms life as a whole, and all the gifts and losses and delights and pains that come with it. Fred wasn't overly depressed and wallowing in the loss of his physical strength, his mental sharpness, or his friends and lovers. He embodied the Nietzschean principle of *amor fati*: he loved his fate and was overflowing with life right up until the end.[2]

To those already familiar with existentialism, it might seem odd to apply this particular brand of philosophy to the phenomenon of aging. We tend to associate "the existentialist" with the commitments of youth, of *doing* rather than *being*, of embracing freedom and rebellion against bourgeois conformism, moral absolutes, and metaphysical security. This figure is often viewed as the embodiment of vitality, courage, and agency, qualities that emerge in the heroic archetype of what the French existentialist Albert Camus branded "the rebel" (*l'homme révolté*). The rebel is the incarnation of "unbounded freedom," someone who is "born of abundance and fullness of spirit" and actively embraces "all that is problematic and strange in our existence."[3] Wearing his signature black sweater and black pants and perhaps smoking a Gauloise cigarette in a Parisian café, he presents a dashing figure, passionate, creative, and wholly engaged in the world. It's no surprise, then, that the weaknesses and vulnerabilities of old age are rarely discussed. Indeed, the only major figure who seriously explores the issue of aging is the French philosopher Simone de Beauvoir, in her work *The Coming of Age*—a massive tome that paints an especially bleak picture of older persons as beings scorned by society, trapped in their bodies, and largely stripped of any kind of meaningful agency. But existentialism is not just a philosophy for the young and healthy. Indeed, the core aim of this short book is to show that existentialism is perhaps most applicable to our later years, as we struggle with illness, physical limitations, the stigmas of our ageist society, and the imminence of death. In fact the true rebel may well be the octogenarian in a wheelchair or a nursing home, not the twenty-year-old nihilist who is drawn to the radical ideas of existentialism but has not yet had to confront the painful realities of life. As the German language poet Rainer Maria Rilke said, the twenty-year-old may grasp the existential questions intellectually, but without the nearness of death and a deep reservoir of life experience to draw from, he or she has not yet learned how to "live the questions."[4]

But what exactly are these questions? It is difficult to answer because the word "existentialism" does not refer to a unified movement or school of thought. There are philosophical and literary existentialists; there are existentialists who believe in God and others, like Nietzsche, who espouse the idea of God's death; and there are some who believe in the existence of free will and others who think that this idea is a moral fiction. Indeed, the term wasn't coined until 1943, long after the nineteenth-century Danish pioneer Søren Kierkegaard laid the conceptual groundwork for it. And of all the major twentieth-century players, only Beauvoir and her compatriot and partner Jean-Paul Sartre self-identified as existentialists. Other like-minded contemporaries disavowed the label for various reasons. Yet for all these disjointed views, there is nonetheless a common set of core principles that binds this diverse group of philosophers and writers together.

The first principle of existentialism is perhaps best captured by Sartre's maxim that "existence precedes essence." This pithy adage suggests that humans are distinct from other creatures in the sense that there is no fixed or pre-given "essence" that ultimately determines or makes us who we are. Humans are self-creating or self-making beings. Unlike my cat, I am not wholly determined by my instincts. I have the capacity to configure my existence through my own situated choices and actions. There is, for this reason, no definitive or complete account of who I am. No matter how old I am, I can always remake or reinterpret myself right up until the moment of death. Existence, then, is not a static thing; it is a dynamic process of becoming, of realizing who we are as we move through the stages of our lives. The existentialist, of course, isn't denying that our inherited compulsions, our physical bodies, and our environmental circumstances limit and constrain us in certain ways. He or she is suggesting, rather, that we are not trapped or determined by these constraints and that what distinguishes us as self-conscious beings is our ability to care for, to reflect on, and to worry about our compulsions, our bodies, and our circumstances, to relate to them and give them meaning. This is why humans are, as Kierkegaard puts it, "a relation that relates to itself."[5] Our ability to relate to ourselves manifests itself in how we choose to interpret and make sense of the limitations and opportunities brought forth by the situation we've been thrown into. The fact that we are free to choose and create our existence in this way is what the existentialist means by "transcendence."

But, insofar as I am self-conscious, I am also painfully

aware that I did not choose to be born and that my being is always threatened by the possibility of non-being, by death. This leads to *the second principle of existentialism*, that the truth of our condition is revealed to us not by means of reason or philosophical reflection but by our emotions and our capacity to feel. When existentialists refer to feelings of "nausea," "anxiety," and "dread," they are trying to capture the gnawing and inchoate sense we have that there is something wrong with us, that there is nothing that ultimately grounds or secures our lives, that there is no reason for us to be at all. Of course, the existentialist also understands that we spend much of our lives fleeing from this painful awareness. We cling to our comfortable routines and social roles; we distract ourselves with gossip and we numb ourselves with intoxicants, soft addictions, and fantasies of an afterlife, all in an effort to escape the feeling of our own groundlessness. But the existentialist makes it clear that the anguish we feel is not something we should recoil from, because it teaches us basic truths about who we are: it teaches us that we are temporal creatures, that our existence is in fact precarious, ambiguous, and uncertain. Understood this way, these unsettling feelings present opportunities for personal growth and transformation; they have the power to shake us out of self-deception and complacency, reminding us of what is truly at stake in our brief and precious lives.

And this leads to *the third principle of existentialism*, that the primary aim of existence is not to experience pleasure or material success. It isn't even to be happy or to be a good person. The aim, rather, is to be *authentic*, to be true to oneself. This means that I should not just conform, or try to fit in with the socially prescribed roles and values of the day. I should commit to the values that give *my* life meaning and that matter to *me* as the unique individual that I am. But one of the keys to being true to oneself is to first recognize that there is no stable self or "I" to begin with, that the very idea, in Nietzsche's words, of an enduring self "is a fiction": one's self "*does not exist at all.*"[6] The first step on the path toward authenticity, then, is to be open and honest with ourselves about our own protean nature and the ambiguity of our condition.

In this book I put forth the idea that it is often easier to be inauthentic and to live in a state of self-deception when we're young and healthy. Brimming with strength and vitality and facing a future wide open to possibilities, we feel secure and invulnerable, as if death wouldn't apply to us. But, as we move into old age, it becomes increasingly difficult to live in denial. The reality of finitude presses in on us every day as our bodies weaken, as illness overtakes us, as friends and family members die. For the older person, as Beauvoir reminds us, "death is no longer a general, abstract fate: it is a personal event, an event that is near at hand."[7] I want to suggest that growing old may actually push us in the direction of authenticity, of facing and accepting the frailty of our existence, and in this way makes it possible to live with a renewed sense of urgency and purpose.

Of course, it is also important not to romanticize the aging process. It is filled with meaningless suffering and loss; it can leave us feeling abandoned, crippled by depression and filled with anger. But the point of this book is to unsettle the common view in our society that old age is some sort of wasting malady or affliction. As American psychologist James Hillman points out, the original meaning of the word "old" has nothing to do with deterioration and decline; it is formed on an Indo-European root that meant "to nourish" and "to be mature"—the same root we find in the Latin *alere* ("to feed, rear, nourish, nurse") and *alimentum* ("nourishment"). To be old, in this light, is to be "fully nourished, grown up, and mature."[8] This may be why the elderly patients in my cardiac rehab appeared to be so different from me. Whereas I was panicked at the thought of coming face to face with death, they were more composed and mature. Nourished by their vast life experience, they seemed better prepared to integrate and accept death into their lives and cherish the limited time they had left.

In the following chapters I try to shed light on a simple idea: that our life is not diminished but enhanced when we are honest and accepting of ourselves as aging and dying. When Rilke refers to the "masterpiece of a long-ripened death," he is pointing out the ways in which growing old can nourish us by releasing us from habituated patterns of self-deception and from the anxieties of denial and can help us come to an awareness of what genuinely matters in our lives. Aging, understood this way, is a long and slow instruction that teaches us the most important lesson: "to learn how to die," how to recognize that the future is an illusion and that all that exists is the beauty and mystery of the present moment, a moment we all too often take for granted in the harried rush of youth and middle age.[9] The autumn of life, then, can be viewed not just as a time of physical decline and infirmity but as one of existential renewal and awakening, a time that allows us to experience what Rilke calls "the ripe fruit of the here and now that has been seized and bitten into and will spread its indescribable taste to us."[10]

1

Death-Man

To see yourself is to die, to die to all illusions.

Søren Kierkegaard

In his classic analysis of the concept of death in children, existential psychotherapist Irvin Yalom describes how youngsters protect themselves by anthropomorphizing death, treating it as if it were something separate from them and giving it a skeletal and ghostly human form. In a conversation with a therapist, Bobby, a four-year-old, says:

[B.] Death does wrong.
[T.] How does it do wrong?
[B.] Stabs you to death with a knife.
[T.] What is death?
[B.] A man.
[T.] What sort of man?
[B.] Death-man.
[T.] How do you know?
[B.] I saw him.[1]

For the existentialist, our childhood fears of "death-man" persist deep into adulthood. Death-man is deteriorating; he is disabled, thin, and frail; he has translucent skin, yellowed and missing teeth, and a stale smell. We don't want to be near death-man because he reminds us of where we are heading. When I was in cardiac rehab I saw many incarnations of death-man, and they terrified me. It was inconceivable that I was like them. But, back on campus a few weeks later, I realized that *I was* death-man. Although the external defibrillator I was wearing after my heart attack to protect me from cardiac arrest was largely concealed under my shirt, it was attached to a camera-sized box at my hip, with a black cord running up my side. It was unmistakably a medical device, and I felt the stigma. I was branded. When colleagues approached me, they would glance uneasily at the device and look at me with concern. What was especially disturbing is that some whom I considered close friends avoided me altogether or would simply smile and scurry away, uncomfortable with what I represented: shattered health, vulnerability, a reminder of death. These jarring experiences forced me to reflect on my obsession with youth, beauty, and strength and my negative views of old age and consider the fact that the pervasiveness of ageism in our culture may manifest itself unconsciously, as a way for us to protect ourselves from the awareness of our own mortality.

The ways in which we belittle and debase the elderly in contemporary society are shocking, especially considering that, at least in the United States, the fastest growing age group is made up of eighty-five- to ninety-four-year-olds.[2] The toxicity of ageism has become acutely visible during the coronavirus pandemic. We have witnessed a remarkably callous attitude toward older persons, as if their lives no longer had any productive value. The

United Kingdom's former political strategist Dominic Cummings remarked that the primary goal of the country's response to the pandemic was to achieve "herd immunity, [to] protect the economy, and if that means some pensioners die, too bad."[3] And Dan Patrick, lieutenant governor of Texas, came under fire for claiming on a nightly news broadcast that, because older persons are no longer contributing members of society, they should be willing to sacrifice their lives for the sake of reopening the economy.[4] These views reflect an attitude that conveys the impression that older persons are neither admired nor respected; they are expendable. And this attitude has become so normalized that it is rarely called into question. Our negative stance toward the elderly appears on the surface not as a subjective expression of bigotry or as a contingent historical quirk so much as an objective fact about the human condition. This is strange because, unlike other "isms" such as sexism or racism, ageism isn't directed at an amorphous "other" with a different gender or skin tone, but at our own future self. Understood this way, ageism looks like a kind of self-hatred of who we will one day become, and this means that older persons today probably participated in the same negative stereotyping that they are now being subjected to. As Beauvoir puts it, "[w]e carry this ostracism so far that we even reach the point of turning it against ourselves: for in the old person that we must become, we refuse to recognize ourselves."[5] This, she says, is "astonishing, since every single member of the community must know that his future is in question."[6]

But in previous eras older persons were not dismissed as incarnations of suffering, illness, and death. Indeed, growing old was viewed as a sign of grace, and mortality was more commonly associated with youth, with dying in childbirth, with injuries from battle, with executions, or with various vocational hazards. The old were regarded as fonts of vitality and wisdom. Their voices mattered because they embodied a deep understanding of the customs, myths, and rituals that held their communities together.[7] This sense of respect and veneration helps us understand the words of the Stoic philosopher Seneca (4 BC–AD 65) in their proper cultural context: "Let us cherish and love old age, for it is full of pleasure if one knows how to use it . . . if God is pleased to add another day, we should welcome it with glad hearts."[8] Contrast Seneca's reflections with the dehumanizing views we have today, when older adults are scorned and functionally removed from productive society, given over to the paternalizing control of medical experts, and warehoused in nursing homes and retirement communities. Beauvoir refers to this phenomenon as nothing less than a "failure of our entire civilization,"[9] but the failure is not merely the byproduct of the unique sociohistorical forces of modern capitalism. The existentialist understands that the segregation of the elderly and the structural discriminations of ageism emerge out of something more insidious and primal: out of our collective fear of death.

Of all the existentialists, none was more haunted by death than Kierkegaard, whose name is homonymous with *kirkegård*, the Danish word for "graveyard." In his brief life of forty-two years, he witnessed the deaths of his parents and of five of his seven siblings; and he had the prophetic belief that he, too, was fated to die at a young age.[10] Kierkegaard was intimately familiar with the abyss that yawns and swirls beneath our lives and recognized this abyss as the wellspring of all our neuroses. He saw death as the ultimate concern, the fundamental given of our existence, and reminded his readers that, although death was certain, the time of death was uncertain; it could come for any of us at any moment. From the standpoint of this "uncertain certainty," he introduced a pioneering distinction between "fear" (*frygt*) and "anxiety" (*angst*) that would later become axiomatic in the development of existential psychotherapy. He argued that fear always has an object; it is always of *something*, and these thing-like fears can be managed and controlled to some extent if we make efforts to avoid them. Anxiety, on the other hand, is a fear of *nothing*; it is fear of the annihilating chasm at the heart of the human condition. Anxiety reveals that there is nothing solid or stable that secures my existence, that I am lost, and that there is no underlying reason for me to be. And I cannot point to what it is that I am anxious about because I *myself* am the source of anxiety. Kierkegaard went on to show that most of our everyday fears manifest themselves as displaced anxiety, whereby the inchoate fear of my own nothingness is transferred onto a more manageable fear of something. My fear of divorce, of losing my job, or of my upcoming colonoscopy displaces and covers over what it is that I'm really afraid of. Kierkegaard believed that, when anxiety is displaced in this way, "the nothing which is the object of anxiety becomes as it were more and more a something."[11]

He goes on to argue that our cultural institutions and social practices are built in large part to repress this anxiety and to keep death hidden from us. Losing ourselves in these practices creates the illusion of well-being, that we are living a good life, that we are not lost, not in despair. In *The Sickness unto Death*, he writes:

> Precisely by losing himself in this way, such a person has gained all that is required for going along superbly in business and social life, yes, for making a great success out of life. Far from anyone thinking him to be in despair, he is just what a human being ought to be. Naturally the world has generally no understanding of what is truly horrifying. The despair that not only does not cause any inconvenience in life but makes life convenient and comfortable is, naturally enough, in no way regarded as despair.[12]

But Kierkegaard believes that this "convenient and comfortable" life is itself the greatest form of despair; it is the despair of self-deception, of "not wanting to be oneself, of wanting to be rid of oneself."[13] And the myriad ways in which we lie to ourselves about death are all too familiar. We believe in the immortality of the soul and an afterlife. We have children, in the hope of living on in them after we're gone. We accumulate wealth, publish books, and produce works of art that will leave a lasting mark. We obsess about fitness and diet and cosmetically alter our physical appearance in our efforts to stay young. We treat aging and death as medical problems that can be solved with new treatments and technologies. We believe in our own specialness: death may happen to others, but it can't possibly happen to me. We even avoid using the word "death" altogether, because of the singular horror it evokes. In his famous story *The Death of Ivan Ilych*, the Russian novelist Leo Tolstoy captures this deep-seated avoidance through his titular character, a shallow everyman suddenly stricken with a terminal illness who is in such a state of denial that he can speak of death only from a detached, third-person standpoint, as a nameless "It" that stalks him. As the illness progresses, his futile attempts to depersonalize death become more desperate.

> Ivan Ilych would turn his attention to it and try to drive the thought of it away, but without success. *It* would come and stand before him and look at him, and he would be horrified, and the light would die out of his eyes, and he would again begin asking himself whether *It* alone was true . . . He would go to his study, lie down, and again be alone with *It*: face to face with *It*. And nothing could be done with *It* except to look at it and shudder.[14]

Ivan Ilych is like all of us, clinging to familiar cultural norms and symbolic practices that shelter us from the terrifying mutability and impermanence of existence. They serve as character defenses that conceal death by creating the appearance that there is something stable, solid, and secure about our lives. Illness and old age are painful exercises in tearing those defenses down and in giving up on the illusion of control. Older persons are frightening to us precisely because they expose our own vulnerability, and we live in a state of denial by pushing them to the margins of our lives. When we mock older persons, we are drawing a clear distinction between "us" and "them." In this way, the rampant ageism we experience today can be regarded as a manifestation of our society's effort to deny and turn away from death. Even media images of so-called "successful aging" are often expressions of this denial, revolving as they do around tropes of autonomy, strength, and mobility. They generally betray the hard realities of growing old, of bodily pain and mental decline, of loss, of being confined to a wheelchair or nursing home. But, more importantly for the existentialist, they point to a deep despair founded on an unwillingness to be honest with ourselves. And Kierkegaard makes it clear that the masquerade is in vain; illness, disability, and death always catch up to us.

> Do you not know that there comes a midnight hour when everyone has to throw off his mask? Do you believe that life will always let itself be mocked? Do you think you can slip away a little before midnight in order to avoid this? Or are you not terrified by it? I have seen men in real life who so long deceived themselves that at last their true nature could not reveal itself.[15]

It is clear that the midnight hour is coming, but here is the trick. For Kierkegaard, we should not recoil from death but earnestly turn toward it, welcome it, and work to integrate it into our lives. Death is our teacher. It is a reminder of our temporal nature, that our time is short, and that our lives cannot be delayed or postponed until tomorrow, next month, or next year. Rilke refers to this attitude as an affirmation of our existence, a state in which we don't run away from death but befriend it, allowing it to "come very close and snuggle up to [us]."[16]

> Believe me that death is a *friend*, maybe the only one who is never, never deterred by our actions and indecision . . . and *this*, you understand, *not* in the sentimental–romantic sense of a denial of life, of the opposite of life, but our friend especially *then* when we most passionately, most tremblingly affirm our being-here . . . Death is the real yes-sayer."[17]

This attitude of affirmation and acceptance is what Kierkegaard means by "earnestness" (*alvor*). It is to live with a sense of seriousness about death, and it is this seriousness that gives our projects a sense of urgency, meaning, and value that they otherwise wouldn't have if we continued to drift along in self-deception, thinking that our time was limitless. "Earnestness," in Kierkegaard's words, "becomes the living of each day as if it were the last and also the first in a long life, and the choosing of work that does not depend on whether one is granted a lifetime to complete it well or only a brief time to have begun it well."[18] When our own death is squarely in view, it enriches the fleeting moments of our lives, allowing us to become fully present to their depth and poignancy. This kind of person, for Kierkegaard, is outwardly unremarkable. In *Fear and Trembling*, he suggests an earnest man could easily be mistaken for a clerk, a shopkeeper, or a postman; there is nothing "aloof or superior" about him. What stands out, however, is that he seems to "take delight in everything he sees."

> He lives as carefree as a ne'er-do-well, and yet he buys up the acceptable time at the dearest price, for he does not do the least thing except by virtue of the absurd . . . Finiteness tastes to him just as good as to one who never knew anything higher.[19]

When Kierkegaard, writing for his nominally Lutheran readers in nineteenth-century Copenhagen, says that the earnest person lives "by virtue of the absurd," he is making it clear that such a person recognizes the fundamental paradox of religious existence, that the divine is not to be found in some otherworldly realm; it is actually bound up in the temporal. It is the finite that has infinite significance. By soberly facing and accepting death, the true Christian experiences the divine *in this life*, and is able to "live joyfully and happily every instant," seeing that each moment might be his or her last.[20] In this way the person recognizes an appalling truth about God: that "he wants you to die, to die unto the world," because dying is a kind of freedom; it liberates us from trivial concerns and distractions and enables us to treasure the moments we have now rather than deferring life to some illusory future.[21] The earnest person knows that we lie to ourselves when we think our happiness is always around the next corner, after the promotion, the wedding, the birth of the child, or the retirement. With death as our most uncertain certainty, all we have is this moment, and the moment is ambiguous; it is not just a cause for anxiety but a cause for joy as well. The German philosopher Martin Heidegger will later develop this idea in *Being and Time*, by writing: "along with the sober anxiety which brings us face to face with our individualized potentiality-for-being, there goes an unshakable joy in this possibility. In it, existence becomes free from the entertaining 'distractions' with which we busy ourselves."[22]

Oncologists and palliative care physicians have long been witnesses to this kind of personal transformation. They have treated terminally ill patients who were initially horrified at their diagnosis but eventually came to view it as liberating. In accepting death, their remaining days often lit up with a sense of urgency and deep meaning; the gravity of their condition pulled them away from frivolous quarrels and ego-driven concerns toward a feeling of gratitude for the short time that was left.

Clinical psychologist Mary Pipher describes a conversation in which an oncologist tells one of his patients: "you are about to experience the most affirming era of your lifetime."[23] Another patient, Kathy, who nearly died of kidney failure, echoes this sentiment, describing her own experience as an existential rebirth.

> The first Kathy died during dialysis. She could not make it long in the face of death. A second Kathy had to be born. This is the Kathy that was born in the midst of death . . .
>
> The first Kathy lived for trivia only. But the second Kathy—that's me now. I am infatuated with life. Look at the beauty of the sky! It's gorgeously blue! I go into a flower garden and every flower takes on such fabulous colors that I am dazzled by their beauty . . . One thing I do know, had I remained the first Kathy, I would have played away my whole life, and I would never have known what the real joy of living was all about. I had to face death eyeball to eyeball before I could live. *I had to die in order to live.*[24]

Kathy has made what Kierkegaard calls a "leap" (*Spring*) into the absurd.[25] Through her dying to the world, the world has come back to her with a depth and an intensity that were missing before her diagnosis. For Kierkegaard, "dying is one of the most remarkable leaps" precisely because it shakes us out of our routinized drift, allows us to see what is really important, and awakens in us a sense of appreciation for simply being alive.[26] This may explain why many terminal patients have referred to their cancer diagnosis positively and, according to Irvin Yalom, sometimes describe it as the best thing that ever happened to them.[27] But we don't need a terminal diagnosis to experience this transformation. We are already terminal, and when we move into the evening of life, the transformation may come more naturally.

This exposes one of the unsettling truths about the coronavirus pandemic. By bringing death clearly into view, it made us realize that we can no longer flee from it. As the world masked up and great cities shut down, as hospitals overflowed with the sick and dying, as we were reminded that a person died from the virus every thirty-three seconds, death ceased to be an impersonal or abstract event.[28] We are all waking up to our own finitude, grappling with the reality that it is now *my life* and *my death* that are at stake. B. J. Miller, a palliative care physician, describes the existential insights that the pandemic has brought to his own dying patients.

> Earlier last week, I had a patient lean into her computer's camera and whisper to me that she appreciates what the pandemic is doing for her: She has been living through the final stages of cancer for a while, only now her friends are more able to relate to her uncertainties, and that empathy is a balm. I've heard many, in hushed tones, say that these times are shaking them into clarity. That clarity may show up as unmitigated sorrow or discomfort, but that is honest and real, and it is itself a powerful sign of life.[29]

The pandemic has pulled away the veil, reminding us how close we are to death at every moment and forcing us to confront the most uncertain certainty that we have spent most of our lives hiding from. It allows us to see, finally, what really matters: not the new car, the job title, or the petty grievance at work but the simple, fleeting delights in life that we ordinarily take for granted. As

Oregon Senator Richard Neuberger wrote just months before he died of cancer,

> Questions of prestige, of political success, of financial status, became all at once unimportant . . . In their stead has come a new appreciation of things I once took for granted—eating lunch with a friend, scratching Muffett's ears and listening for his purrs, the company of my wife, reading a book in the quiet cone of my bed lamp at night . . . For the first time I think I'm actually savoring life.[30]

When we are young and healthy, we are, in Kierkegaard's words, often "too tenacious of life to die."[31] But this tenacious grip begins to loosen as we grow older and move closer to death; we begin to let go of the temporal and, by virtue of the absurd, the temporal comes back to us and is now illuminated in ways it never was before. Kierkegaard calls this a "double movement" (*dobbeltbevaegelse*), a movement whereby "every instant we see the sword hanging over the head" and are overcome not only with terror but with awe, as we marvel at the majesty and richness of the moment.[32] John Leland noticed this deep wisdom in his study of the elderly. Jonas Mekas, one of the New Yorkers with whom Leland spent more than one year, was a ninety-two-year-old Lithuanian immigrant who survived the horrors of the Nazi concentration camps and lived with an unblinking acceptance of death and an awareness that the future was an illusion. He appeared to embrace Kierkegaard's paradox, that the finite has infinite significance, that the eternal is not to be found in some supersensible realm but is right here, in the present. After experiencing so much loss in his long life, he describes the simple delights of the temporal that we assume will always be there for us, like eating a plate of grapes. "This plate is my Paradise," he says. "I don't want anything else—no country house, no car, no dacha, no life insurance, no riches. It's this plate of grapes that I want. It's this plate of grapes that makes me really happy. To eat my grapes and enjoy them and want nothing else—that is happiness, that's what makes me happy."[33]

Jonas sees death-man in the mirror, but doesn't recoil from what he sees. He has no illusions and embodies the Kierkegaardian spirit of earnestness. Jonas knows that the clock is ticking, but it is this knowledge that each fleeting moment could be his last, that this grape may be the last sweet thing he tastes, that gives meaning and clarity to his life. Kierkegaard describes this state as being "awakened" to who we are and to what we really care about; it is "to be wide awake and to think death ... to think that all was over, that everything was lost along with life," but to do so "in order to win everything in life."[34] Awakened in this way, Jonas lives with a sense of urgency and vitality that is missing in folks half his age. In the winter of his life, he embodies the core truth of Kierkegaard's philosophy: that "death in earnest gives life force as nothing else does; it makes one alert as nothing else does."[35]

2

Letting Go

Above all, don't lie to yourself.

Fyodor Dostoevsky

When I had my heart attack in the winter of 2017, I was finishing up a sixty-mile bike ride, something I did regularly on weekends. I had long prided myself on my athleticism and fitness and spent much of my youth playing sports and hiking and skiing in the Rocky Mountains. As I drifted into an academic career and into middle age, I moved away from the high peaks but continued a vigorous exercise program at the gym, on racquetball courts, and on my road bike. Seeing myself through the prism of physical strength created the comforting illusion that there was something secure and thing-like about my existence, that I was solid and invulnerable. This view extended to how I saw myself in the classroom: as a passionate and dynamic teacher, who could engage students for hours at a time with lively and animated lectures. This self-interpretation all came crashing down with my failing heart. After leaving the intensive care unit at the hospital and in the days and weeks that followed, I could barely walk to the end of the block without losing my breath, and the various blood pressure and arrhythmia medications made me light-headed and fatigued in front of my students. It felt as if the ground beneath me was collapsing as I confronted the reality that I was no longer the person I used to be. This forced me to face the difficult question of who the "true" or "real" me actually was. If I am not a strong, healthy, and energetic college professor, *who am I*?

For the existentialist, human existence is not a determinate thing; it is the activity or process of self-creation, and we become who we are only on the basis of the situated choices and actions we make as our lives unfold. This means that human existence is always on the way, always "not yet," as we ceaselessly fashion and refashion ourselves against the constraints and limitations of life. When we leave home for the first time, when we graduate from college, when we get married and start a family, when we retire from work, we are forever running up against new constraints and limitations and must continually re-create ourselves in their midst. This is what distinguishes us from other animals. As the Spanish existentialist José Ortega y Gasset writes, "our being consists not in what it is already, but in what it is *not yet*, a being that consists in *not-yet-being*. Everything else in the world is what it is . . . Man is the entity that makes itself . . . He has to determine *what* he is going to be."[1] Ortega y Gasset is not suggesting here that there are no facts that determine us as human beings. It is a fact, for instance, that I was born a man, or that I am—at least for the time being—ambulatory and able-bodied, or that I am shaped and influenced by my historical situation and my relationships with others. What is unique to human existence is that we are self-aware, we are conscious of these facts; we can relate to them, worry about them, and make decisions about how to cope with them or change them in the future. We exist, in Ortega y Gasset's words, "half immersed in nature, half transcending it."[2] Our life unfolds as an ambiguous tension between the givens (or "facticity") of our lives and our ability to rise above or transcend these givens by choosing to interpret them and act on them in certain ways. As an expression of the struggle between "facticity" and "transcendence," we can always negate whatever determines us as a particular kind of person; and we can do so by reflecting on these determinations, questioning them, and giving them new meanings in light of future projects. In other words, although we are always products of our environments, we are also free to change. We are both self-making and already made. As the French philosopher Maurice Merleau-Ponty puts it, "[w]e exist in both ways at once. We choose the world and the world chooses us."[3]

For me, this meant that the secure sense I had of myself was an illusion all along. Unlike a rock or a tree, I am not identical with myself: this is because I can freely choose to relate to my situation in different ways. I could hold on to the self-interpretation that I had built up over many years; or I could let go of it and work to refashion a new identity. My heart attack made this structural instability clear to me and helped me truly understand what Sartre meant when he said that "human existence is constituted as a being which is what it is not and which is not what it is."[4] The problem, of course, is that I didn't want to let go. I was still clinging to the past and the thing-like shelter of my former self, unwilling to accept the fissure of "nothingness" whirring beneath me. I grasped at comforting falsehoods conveyed by friends, colleagues, and physicians that I was not going to die, that I'd have a full recovery, that everything would be fine. I refused to see and acknowledge what was staring me in the face, that my being is already vulnerable and unstable (in Sartre's words, "metastable"), and that any sense of who I am is "always subject to sudden changes and transitions" that are based on how I understand my future projects and the contingent givens of my life.[5]

To the existentialist, my response to the crisis was not indicative of a moral failing. "The lie," as Sartre says, "is a normal phenomenon" and self-deception is inescapable; it is built into who we are.[6] We deny the annihilating aspect of our condition because it exposes us to the dizzying freedom and uncertainty that lurk behind our curated personas. To be human, then, is to be in "bad faith" (*mauvaise foi*), a kind of inauthenticity that manifests itself either in denying our freedom and holding fast to the illusion that our being is unambiguously thing-like and secure or in denying the contingent givens of our situation and thinking that we are completely free and undetermined. To be honest or true to ourselves, then, requires a kind of clear-sighted acceptance of the instability and ambiguity at the core of existence. But it is more than this. For Sartre, it also requires an ability to be flexible and fluid, to change and "adapt one's life" to the unavoidable shocks and upheavals.[7] This is a kind of wisdom that old age can bring. As we move into our later years, we become increasingly aware that the identities we worked so hard to establish and maintain were fragile all along. The fortifications of the self that we spend decades building through our careers, through spouses and children, through homes and savings accounts are all exposed as gossamer. The things that provide us with our sense of who we are disappear one by one as we age—when we retire from work, when friends and family die, when we're placed in a long-term care facility, when the body begins its steep descent into senescence. In the wake of these losses, we are forced to confront ourselves, to let go of the myth of control and self-certainty, and to adapt and improvise as former lives become unlivable. And this sense of plasticity embodied in a willingness to give up on, and let go of, former selves helps us better understand what the existentialist means by "authenticity."

The call to be authentic has deep roots in the West that can be traced back to ancient Greece and a maxim inscribed on the portico at the Temple of Apollo in Delphi: "know thyself." The maxim reminds us of how important it is to see that your existence and its unique tangle of traits, desires, experiences, and failings belong to *you* and express what *you are*.[8] This is to see ourselves, as the Spanish existentialist Miguel de Unamuno writes, "as unique and irreplaceable; there cannot be any other I . . . no one else can fill the gap that will be left when we die." To be authentic, on this view, is to "make yourself irreplaceable," to choose yourself and exist in a way that is genuine and true to the things that matter to you as an individual.[9] And one of the consistent criticisms that the existentialist levels against modern mass society is that we are often unwilling to be authentic, to commit ourselves to the idiosyncratic concerns that are important to us. Instead, we simply drift along and conform with the crowd, living, in Nietzsche's words, as "herd animals" (*Herdentiere*) and lacking the courage and strength to lead our own lives.[10] But as we move into our later years we tend to become less concerned with fitting in or with the approval of the crowd. We age into our own uniqueness, becoming more resilient, more comfortable with the skein of eccentricities that make us who we are.[11]

But, in the existentialist's view, having the fortitude to express or live these eccentricities does not mean that we possess some kind of transparent knowledge of who we are. As Nietzsche reminds us, "to become what one is presupposes that one not have the faintest notion of what one is."[12] Indeed, as we move into old age and slowly unspool the tangled threads of the self, we don't arrive at clarity at all. We often find ourselves swimming in ambiguity and mystery. At the end of his autobiography, the Swiss psychiatrist Carl Jung writes: "I am astonished, disappointed, pleased with myself. I am distressed, depressed, rapturous. I am all these things at once, and I cannot add up the sum . . . I have no judgment about myself and my life. There is nothing I am quite sure about." But this confusion is not experienced as despair. By then in his eighties, Jung felt more comfortable and at home in the fundamental unsettledness of who he was. "The more uncertain I have felt about myself," he writes, "the more there has grown up in me a feeling of kinship with all things."[13] On this account, being true to oneself in old age involves letting go of the illusion of self-certainty altogether, and a willingness to face and accept the underlying mystery of existence. Heidegger develops this idea in his own account of authenticity.

Of all the major figures, it is undoubtedly Heidegger who offered the most influential and comprehensive account of authenticity, spending much of the second half of his masterwork *Being and Time* exploring the topic. He employs the abstract noun *Eigentlichkeit*, formed on the stem of the adjective *eigen* ("own" or "proper"), which means literally "(the property of) being one's own" or, more simply, "ownness." To be authentic, then, is to be true to one's own self, which, as we now see, is fundamentally unsettled to begin with. In the course of everyday life we tend to be "inauthentic" (*uneigentlich*); we disown ourselves, recoiling from our own unsettledness and fleeing back into the false security of our public personas. But these attempts become more difficult as we move into old age. The well-worn masks that kept the truth hidden for so many years no longer work as the future closes down and we run up against our temporal limits. For Heidegger, this confrontation requires a steadiness and focus that he calls "resoluteness" (*Entschlossenheit*), but this term is often misunderstood as conveying a sense of being unyielding and stubborn, a kind of soldierly and masculine attitude, as if the authentic individual were akin to an existential stormtrooper with the resolve and courage to charge headlong into the void. When Heidegger describes resoluteness as a kind of "taking action," "steadiness," and "being ready for death," the image of a frail octogenarian is not one that readily comes to mind.[14] But this is a mistake, and if we look closely at how Heidegger employs the word we can see why.

Entschlossenheit is a compound of *schliessen* ("to close"), preceded by *ent-* (an inseparable verbal prefix that indicates mainly privation, reversal, and beginning); and Heidegger uses this word to capture the literal sense of being unlocked, open, and receptive to the inherent vulnerability and ambiguity of existence. It is a word that refers to the importance of being loose and ready to both adapt to how we interpret ourselves and let go of identities and ways of being that can no longer be sustained. This means that, if I am to be authentic, whoever it is that I choose to be at any given time, I have to simultaneously *"hold"* that identity *"free* for the possibility of *taking it back."*[15] Resoluteness, understood this way, is an anticipatory attitude, indicating that an individual is prepared and ready to die. But death, here, is not a reference to the end of biological life or of physical perishing. It points rather to a kind of ego death, the loss of one's self-identity, a state in which we find ourselves disconnected and unmoored from the world and unable to understand or make sense of who we are. "To exist," for Heidegger, "is essentially to understand," to embody a seamless and tacit familiarity with the people and things we deal with in everyday life.[16] As we move into old age, this background understanding of things begins to fray and breaks down, because the meanings offered up by our youth-obsessed world no longer apply or resonate to us. We die, in Heidegger's words, because "the 'world' can offer nothing more," and this "takes away the possibility of understanding ourselves."[17] Rather than stubbornly clinging to the false security of the identities we fashioned in youth and middle age, authentic aging demands resoluteness, a focused readiness to die that frees us from the grip of egoistic striving and opens up what Heidegger calls a *Spielraum* ("play space"), a space or margin of freedom, releasement, and letting go. In *Being and Time* he describes this inner space as a kind of existential maturity that reveals itself in one's willingness *"to give up on oneself* and thus shatter all one's tenaciousness to whatever existence one has reached."[18]

This theme of ego death is developed more fully in Heidegger's later writings and in his meditations on *Gelassenheit*, a word commonly translated as "equanimity" or "serenity." But, in a debt to Meister Eckart (1260–1328), the famous German mystic and theologian, Heidegger focuses on the literal sense of the verb *lassen* ("to allow," "let," "release"). Understood from this angle, *Gelassenheit* acquires a twofold meaning. It signals both a releasement from the willful, ego-driven concerns that create the illusion of the self as something solid and enduring, and an openness to and acceptance of the fundamental mystery and uncertainty of existence. It is an attitude that, in Heidegger's words, "demands of us not to cling one-sidedly to a single idea" and opens us up to the possibility of a "being loosened" (*Losgelassensein*) from our attachments to things, careers, social status, material possessions, and physical appearance.[19] Detaching from and letting go of these egoistic preoccupations allows us to become more comfortable with our own nothingness. As Meister Eckhart writes, "[f]or whoever would be this or that wants to be *something*, but detachment wishes to be *nothing*."[20] In his year-long study of elderly New Yorkers, John Leland witnessed the wisdom of *Gelassenheit*. He was often struck by the absence of willful and egoistic striving and by how rarely these elders discussed their professional accomplishments, the obstacles they had to overcome, or the amount of time they had spent working or building their careers. What became most evident was their remarkable ability to improvise, to let go and adapt in the face of change, grief, and loss.[21]

Leland saw this in Ping Wong, a ninety-year-old immigrant with crippling arthritis who lived on food stamps, supplemental security benefits, and Medicaid and could still speak only rudimentary English after many decades of living in the United States. When she discussed the myriad experiences of grief and hardship in her long life, she spoke of them with a kind of serene acceptance. "It takes your heart," she said. "But it can happen. Too smooth a life is not very good. You train your brain to deal with difficult challenges. When it passes, just let it go by. Next time, learn from it. I learn something from loss. If you never met something bad, you don't know how to deal with it when you do."[22] Leland was awed by Ping's ability to adapt and be flexible, to "just let it go by," as well as by her capacity to distinguish what really mattered in life from those superficial attachments (or "false needs") that we spend so much of our time obsessing about. "When I compared my life with Ping's," wrote Leland, "I was struck by how many 'needs' I had that she managed to live without: professional accomplishment, parental approval, my marriage, time at the gym, the right microgreens from the farmers market, an apartment that cost too much. They didn't matter as much as I thought they did."[23] Leland recognized that Ping's capacity to let go of false needs and accept the upheavals and emergencies of life led her to a mature and nuanced sense of happiness.

When we are young, we tend to think that happiness has something to do with pleasure or feeling good. But this attitude all too often puts us on "the hedonic treadmill," as psychologists describe it—a place where we are pulled into an empty cycle of chasing our desires, endlessly searching for the next pleasure without any sense of the overarching meaning or purpose of this pleasure-seeking behavior. And, as Leland points out, this cycle is often conditional, such that one is happy "if only" certain conditions are met. If only I were promoted at work; if only I made more money; if only I had a bigger house, a slimmer body, or a newer car. But, for the existentialist, life is never completely good (or completely bad). It is neither and it is both; it is always ambiguous, unstable, and uncertain. This is why Ping says: "When you're young, you don't know what you mean by happiness or sadness."[24] Being able to come to terms with the givens of growing old and to be released from hedonistic concerns in order to focus on what is genuinely important is the kind of wisdom that Ping appeared to possess. And these capacities reveal one of the paradoxes of growing old, namely one that goes against so many of the ageist stereotypes in our culture: it is possible that we become more satisfied and open when we move into our later years because we finally begin to see what is at stake in life. The inevitable experiences of grief, loss, and vulnerability are, as Rilke puts it, "an unsparing way of placing us on intimate and trusting terms with that side of our existence that is turned away from us."[25] Social psychologists who work in the field of socioemotional selectivity theory have noticed this pattern in studies of the elderly where it is found that older adults are often able to maintain more positive emotions than their more youthful and productive counterparts, not just because they are more comfortable with ambiguity but because they are far more selective in their commitments and projects and invest more in interpersonal relationships and forms of communication that are intimate and honest.[26] And if we examine the temporal structure of existence, we may see that this shift emerges naturally.

According to existentialists, time is not to be understood as something separate or independent from us; it is not a datable sequence of "now" points that can be located on a clock or a calendar. Clock time is actually parasitic on a more primordial conception of existential or lived time. And lived time is not something that human existence has; it is *who we are*. "Time is existence," says Heidegger, "and existence is time."[27] From the perspective of aging, then, time has little to do with one's chronological age, or even with the periods of changing biological processes—menopause, erectile dysfunction, or cognitive decline. It is rather a reference to a future that is narrowing or contracting, forcing out projects and possibilities that are no longer livable. This idea of temporal contraction is perhaps best grasped with the help of Heidegger's cryptic rendering of existence as a "thrown projection" (*geworfen Entwurf*). To be human is to be contingently "thrown" into an embodied, socio-historical situation that we can't put behind us, and it is against the background of this situation that a future opens up, revealing a horizon of possibilities that we can "project" for ourselves. We come to understand and make sense of who we are through these historically mediated projects. When Heidegger says that "[w]e are thrown into the kind of being which we call projecting," he is describing how our existence or self-understanding is always "running ahead" of itself, pressing forward into possibilities but always against the constraints and limitations of our past.[28] Thus, in Heidegger's words, "running ahead to the past is our possibility of Being";

it "is time itself."[29]

When we are young and healthy, the horizon of future projects is expansive, revealing a broad range of possibilities that we can press into. Whether it is choosing a new career, changing relationship status, learning a new sport, or moving to a different part of the country, the future promises a nearly limitless array of options through which we can fashion and refashion ourselves. At this stage in life, our orientation is largely acquisitive, shaped by a desire for pleasure, novelty, and adventure. Heidegger refers to this attitude as "curiosity" (*Neugier*), a state in which we are carried away by these desires, "seeking novelty only in order to leap from it anew to another novelty."[30] This acquisitive attitude generally assumes that the future is open and broad. But, as we age, our expansive future begins to contract, gradually closing off possibilities that are no longer viable. This experience of contraction can be terrifying, triggering an awareness of our finitude and often bringing about the so-called midlife crisis.

This kind of crisis is, of course, a relatively recent phenomenon, in large part owing to a dramatic change in the average life span in the West. In the late nineteenth century, for example, the life expectancy was about forty years, and one's adult life was devoted largely to work, marriage, and raising children. By the time the last child left the house, the parents were already close to death, if not dead already. As psychologist Elizabeth Stine-Morrow suggests, "[w]e don't know how to be old because old age is relatively young."[31] Today the life expectancy for Americans is near eighty; this is ample time to reflect on one's contracting future. Such reflections can result in predictable midlife behaviors—

from newfound obsessions with nutrition, exercise, and losing weight, in an effort to look and feel younger and more vital, to behaviors dictated by the depressing feeling of being trapped, be it in the same job for another twenty years before retirement or in a marriage that has been stripped of the essential meanings associated with child rearing. One woman writes:

> It's unbelievable when I think of it now. I never really saw past about age forty-two, where I am now. I mean I never thought about what happens to the rest of life. Pretty much the whole adult life was supposed to be around your husband and raising children. Dammit, what a betrayal! Nobody ever tells you that there's many years of life after children are raised. Now what?[32]

Although forty-two is hardly old, the crisis of meaning this woman is describing and the myriad age-denying behaviors that begin to appear in midlife may be the response to a dormant anxiety, which erupts when a contracting future reveals our essential finitude. For the existentialist, as I have shown, these crises have the power to disclose fundamental truths about the human condition. On this view, the woman's anxiety is directed not at her new life without children to look after, but at her own structural unsettledness. The crisis reveals that any sense of stability and constancy regarding the identity she has established for herself after many years of mothering was a conceit. When her children left home, the meaning and coherence of her identity were stripped away. She was exposed to her own contingency, to the fact that there is nothing enduring or certain about her being.

From this perspective, growing old can be viewed and

experienced as a kind of liberation from the illusion of our own permanence. Our obsessions with money, family, social status, and physical appearance that serve to sustain the illusion in youth and in middle age become increasingly irrelevant as we move into our later years. When the future closes down and we are confronted with our own mortality, we come to recognize that there was no enduring or stable self to begin with and that we are, at bottom, a finite existence, a fundamentally vulnerable and tenuous process of self-creation. Following Heidegger's lead, psychiatrist Irvin Yalom found that when his elderly patients accepted this truth, they often felt freer and less constricted in their lives. They came to recognize that their anxiety emerged from avoiding their own impermanence rather than from facing it.[33] When they were capable of *Gelassenheit*, of letting go of the ego, their lives opened up and their experiences deepened with a renewed sense of urgency and purpose. When asked by a patient to reflect on his own impermanence in the twilight of his life, Yalom admits: "I have my 3 a.m. bouts with anxiety about dying too, but they occur far less now, and, as I grow older, gazing at death has some positive results: I feel more poignancy, more vitality in my life; death makes me live more in each moment—valuing and appreciating the sheer pleasure of awareness, of being alive."[34] The lesson, for Yalom, is that old age has the power to release us from the illusion of the self and the ego-driven fears and distractions that come with it. And when this happens, we receive something profound and powerful in return, that is, the simple delight of being.

3

A Chasm of Stillness

The old person is condemned to boredom.

Simone de Beauvoir

In her book *The Coming of Age*, Beauvoir refers to "boredom" (*ennui*) as the dominant mood in old age. Often warehoused in nursing homes or in retirement communities, in states of cognitive and physical decline, stripped of their usefulness and of the preoccupations of work, older persons are left to drift along, in indifference. "There is nothing left that interests or stirs them," she writes. "They have no projects anymore; they see the world as so much pasteboard scenery and themselves as living corpses."[1] Because they are "no longer directed to any aims nor faced with any requirements," they are forced to confront a chasm of stillness that their active younger selves could avoid.[2] But, for existentialists (and this includes Beauvoir), the way we turn away from boredom by busying ourselves in everyday social life reveals something about who we are. Kierkegaard refers to the restless mass as the "public" (*offentligheden*); Nietzsche calls it "the herd" (*die Herde*); and Heidegger refers to "the they" (*das Man*). When we are pulled along by the bustling crowd, "we take pleasure and enjoy ourselves as *they* take pleasure. We read, see, and judge about literature and art as *they* see and judge ... we find shocking what *they* find shocking. The 'they' ... prescribes the kind of being of everydayness."[3] By engaging in public life and immersing ourselves in work, travel, shopping, and gossip we are able to cover over our boredom and the emptiness that whirs beneath us. Heidegger describes this manner of acting as a kind of restlessness motivated by an "inability to bear the stillness" of our own lives.[4] In this state of "untrammeled, explosive rushing," we are in constant motion, craving diversion, and carried away by the novelties of the day. He refers to this state simply as "busyness" (*der Betrieb*); it is a state in which we are literally "driven away" (*angetrieben*) from ourselves by the frenzy of incessant activity. This acquisitive way of being is often characteristic of life in youth and in middle age and presupposes a measure of health, an able body, and an experience of time that is open and expansive. But, with retirement and the loss of mobility, strength, and cognitive dexterity that comes with aging, it becomes increasingly difficult to abandon oneself to the buzzing commotion of modern life. The result is a confrontation with stillness that can be deeply unsettling.

Before my heart attack, I was the incarnation of busyness, perpetually on the go and driven by a kind of kinetic agitation. My life was organized and regulated by ceaseless activity and the imperative of getting things done. I would run from the classroom to the office, to the gym, to the restaurant, to the airport, all in an effort to avoid confronting stillness. Weekends and holidays were often frightening because I would have to face stretches of time that were unstructured and formless. To cope with this, I made my laptop and my iPhone constant companions, making it possible to distract myself with work or my addiction to social media. In this way, I could always flee from feelings of indifference and emptiness. But on medical leave, immobilized and bed ridden, I came face-to-face with the source of my restlessness, and it was terrible. It became clear to me that my anguish was not, in Heidegger's words, "caused by a conspicuous event or set of circumstances." What I was suffering from was more inconspicuous, diffused, and atmospheric; it was an "all-consuming boredom" that emerged from an inability to distract or escape from myself.[5]

In his *Pensées* (*Thoughts*), the famous French philosopher and mathematician Blaise Pascal (1623–1662), who is sometimes labeled a proto-existentialist, explores the nature of this wretched state. In a section headed "Diversion," he suggests that our confrontation with emptiness is painful because of our own confusion about the good life. We think that amusement, excitement, and pleasure are what makes us happy. But the word "diversion," although it commonly signifies "distraction," has its roots in the Latin *divertere*, which means to "turn aside," "turn away from," or "turn against," and it is this etymological sense that Pascal focuses on. My nonstop preoccupation with things was an attempt to evade or turn away from the nothingness at the core of my existence. To use Pascal's mode of thinking, it was not the stillness of boredom that made me miserable. My misery emerged from a diverted life, entrenched in the inability to be quiet and still. "The only thing that consoles us from our miseries," writes Pascal, "is diversion. And yet it is diversion that is the greatest of our miseries. For it is that above all which prevents us from thinking about ourselves and leads us imperceptibly to destruction."[6] This means that the quivering unease I experienced during my convalescence arose from "one single fact," that is, my "inability to sit quietly in a room alone."[7] All the things that I had spent my life running away from were now exposed: "nullity, loneliness, inadequacy, dependence, helplessness, emptiness." But, for Pascal, these things are the very givens of existence.[8] By running away from them we run away from who we are. Pascal reminds his readers that restlessness is itself a form of despair and that the aim of the good life is to learn how to befriend our own boredom, to slow down, to be empty, silent, and still. It is only then that we can come to understand the lesson that "to live quietly is to live happily."[9]

Here Pascal is making the strange case that we don't really want peace and tranquility in our lives. We are afraid of them because they force us to confront ourselves. "Man finds nothing so intolerable as to be in a state of complete rest, without passions, without occupation, without diversion, without effort."[10] But, unless we confront such a state, we continue to suffer; we remain lost and estranged from ourselves. Existentialists have played an important role in explaining how this manifestation of suffering is exacerbated today, because modern life has created increasingly sophisticated ways to manufacture distractions and to satisfy our cravings for novelty. In his *Contributions to Philosophy*, Heidegger will refer to this unsettled state as a form of "acceleration" (*Schnelligkeit*), and considers it one of the signature symptoms of the technological age, where we are always caught up in the "mania for what is surprising, for what immediately sweeps away and impresses, again and again in different ways."[11] But being sped up and distracted in this way actually contributes to our own boredom, because we are unable to make qualitative distinctions among the choices and commitments that really matter to us. This style of living is, for Heidegger, a kind of "self-forming emptiness."[12] In our fragmented and harried state, everything is equally important because nothing stands out, nothing matters. All we do is pass the time with the various things that occupy and distract us, and life is organized around the principle of "driving away whatever is boring" by filling up the emptiness in us with unabated activity.[13] And Heidegger makes it clear that this activity is self-defeating, because we are fundamentally indifferent to the very things we busy ourselves with. In the era of acceleration, then, "nothing appeals to us anymore, because everything has as much or as little value as everything else."[14]

Although Heidegger's words capture the gadget-driven emptiness of the digital age and anticipate many of the critical terms that social theorists use nowadays to describe this phenomenon—terms such as infoglut, data smog, analysis paralysis, and information fatigue syndrome—it was actually Kierkegaard who pioneered the existentialist takedown of modern busyness.[15] In *Either/Or*, he famously employs an agricultural metaphor that he calls "the rotation method" as a way to escape boredom. Just as the farmer must constantly change or "rotate" the crops to keep the soil fertile, the busy person seeks continual change and newness to combat indifference and to revitalize and refresh his or her experience. But this way of living is ultimately futile and leads to despair, because we become trapped in a vicious cycle of searching for novel experiences while the underlying meaning or purpose of this search is never addressed.

> One tires of living in the country, and moves to the city; one tires of one's native land, and travels abroad; one is tired of Europe, and goes to America, and so on . . . One tires of porcelain dishes and eats on silver; one tires of silver and turns to gold; one burns half of Rome to get an idea of the burning of Troy. This method defeats itself; it is plain endlessness.[16]

The busy person lives a life that is "divided and scattered," pulled apart by a multiplicity of distractions.[17] "He sows and harvests and again sows and harvests (busyness harvests over and over again) . . . and [then] rests upon these gains." But what is the point of all this? It is simply an attempt to flee from the boredom that washes over us when we're "standing still."[18] For Kierkegaard, the problem with this way of living is that boredom is diffused and indeterminate; busying ourselves with things is in vain, because our indifference is not directed at a specific object or experience. It is not as if we were bored with an uninteresting book, a droning philosophy lecture, or the empty stretch of time as we wait for the plane to depart. We are bored *with everything*, with our existence as a whole, and we cannot escape it by means of busyness because we ourselves are the source of it. "Boredom," as Kierkegaard reminds us, "rests upon *the nothing* that binds our existence together."[19] This helps us understand his claim that the busy person is "the most boring of all, and if they are not bored, it is because they do not know what boredom is."[20]

According to Kierkegaard, in order to identify what is truly at stake in life, we need to be patient, to still ourselves, and to pay attention to the choices and commitments that define us and make us who we are. On this account, idleness is not to be viewed as a sin that ceaseless work absolves us from. Idleness is rather the only path to "a truly divine life."[21] And it is a path that opens up to us as we move into old age and let go of the frenzied world of work and distraction. If we have the courage to accept and integrate stillness into our lives, the diminution of aging can be viewed as a liberation or rebirth rather than a sign of physical decay and diminishment. Aging forces us to slow down, and this allows us to be attentive to the fleeting and poignant beauty of what is right in front of us, to see the world with eyes that are fresh and new, the eyes of a beginner. Frances, a nursing home resident, describes this experience as a kind of personal awakening.

> Lack of physical strength keeps me inactive and often silent. They call me senile, but senility is just a convenient peg on which to hang non-conformity. A new set of faculties seems to be coming into operation. More than any other time of my life I seem to be aware of the beauties of our spinning planet and the sky above. Old age is sharpening my awareness.[22]

In Kierkegaard's words, Frances has been released from a preoccupation with things and has learned how to be still, that is, *nil admirari*, be surprised at nothing, which, he says, "is the proper wisdom of life."[23]

This idea, of a rebirth or new beginning that emerges when we step out of the endless cycle of busyness, is a recurring one in the existentialist tradition. It explains what the Jewish philosopher Martin Buber meant when, at the end of his life, he wrote: "to be old is a glorious thing when one has not unlearned what it means *to begin*. This old man had perhaps first learned it thoroughly in old age."[24] Heidegger echoes Buber's sentiments in his later writings, describing this rebirth as a way of living in "the nearness" (*die Nähe*). This is a kind of contemplative or mindful attentiveness in which we are able to "dwell on what lies close and to meditate on what is closest; upon that which concerns us, each one of us, here and now; here, on this patch of home ground; now, in the present hour of history."[25] Rather than filling the stillness of our lives with distractions, Heidegger encourages an "expectant decisiveness to be patient" and "the courage to go slowly."[26] Growing old in this way can pull us out of our agitation and draw us into the moment-to-moment experiences that we so often took for granted when we were speeding through life. In slowly and patiently attending to what is near, the most ordinary thing—a conversation with a friend, a cup of coffee in the morning, the cat purring on the couch, or a thunderstorm in spring—can be experienced as "extraordinary" (*erstaunlich*). It is an attitude that, in Heidegger's words, "sets us before the ordinary itself," but "precisely as what is the most extraordinary."[27] By slowing down we become aware of the incredible fragility and impermanence of ordinary things.

The resonance with Buddhism is striking. One of the core insights of Buddhist philosophy is the recognition that our anguish or "suffering" (*dukkha*) is grounded in a longing for life to be other than what it is: fleeting, unreliable, impermanent. Our conditioned restlessness allows us to hide or turn away from who we are. But, like the existentialist, the Buddha reminds us of our situation: "No conditions are permanent; No conditions are reliable; Nothing is self."[28]

The problem is that, when we are caught up in this evasive way of being, it eventually becomes a habit, so that our lives are lived on a kind of autopilot; they are reflexively conditioned by busyness and they turn away from the truth that nothing is self, forgetting it. Pulled along by our attachments to money, to work, to possessions, to health and fitness, this conditioning becomes entrenched and all-encompassing; it bleeds into every aspect of life and deepens the confusion we have about who we are and what we are supposed to do. As the Buddha says, "[c]onfusion conditions activity, which conditions consciousness, which conditions embodied personality, which conditions sensory experience, which conditions mood, which conditions craving, which conditions clinging, which conditions becoming, which conditions birth, which conditions aging and death."[29] In this way, the compulsive agitation and distractibility, what the Buddhist calls "the monkey mind," becomes the default setting of our lives; and this represents the deepest and most profound form of suffering—a suffering that is so inconspicuous, pervasive, and wide-ranging that we forget we are suffering. Heidegger refers to this situation as the most "urgent distress" (*nötigende Not*), one where busyness and distraction come "to be accepted and practiced *as the only way of being*."[30]

In order to come to terms with our own nothingness, we have to somehow decondition ourselves from this automatic and unconscious way of being. The French existentialist Gabriel Marcel explores this problem in his work *Being and Having*, suggesting that we live in "a broken world" (*un monde cassé*) because we have become enslaved to the "having" mode. We see our self-worth bound up with our possessions, our social status, our attractiveness and physical bodies. It is a compulsive and egoistic mode grounded in desiring, wanting, and seizing; and it invariably leads to despair.[31] "The more we allow ourselves to be servants of Having," writes Marcel, "the more we shall let ourselves fall prey to the oppressive anxiety which Having involves."[32] He reminds us that existence (or "being") is not something we have; it is not a problem to be solved or a possession to be acquired. Being just is *to be*. It is "nothingness . . . the grand mystery."[33] To enter into the "being" mode we have to learn how to free ourselves from "the armor of Having, which covers us: the armor of our possessions, our attainments, our experiences and our virtues, perhaps even more than our vices."[34] Old age may provide a natural release from the anguish of having, allowing us to slow down, to be present, and attend to the concerns that really matter. The Buddhist existentialist Stephen Batchelor makes this point, understanding that this kind of liberation or awakening doesn't occur overnight; it is a lifelong process, a maturation that enables us to finally blow out the fires of our own restlessness and to grow toward an acceptance of the nothing at the heart of existence.

It will probably take place over a substantial period of time, during which it is nurtured by certain "key" experiences (insight into one's own mortality, for example) before becoming crystallized in a conscious realization or an overt act . . . We are left with no choice but to shift the center of our personal life from the dimension of Having to that of Being. This produces a sense of joyous inner release and freedom from the gnawing uneasiness of our previous vacillation.[35]

In *The Gay Science*, Nietzsche develops this idea of joy in being released from busyness and warns his readers of the unique harms that are inflicted when existence is conditioned by "the breathless haste" of modernity. In an aphorism entitled "Leisure and Idleness," he challenges the cult of distraction, writing: "even now one is ashamed of resting, and prolonged reflection almost gives people a bad conscience. One thinks with a watch in one's hand, even as one eats one's midday meal while reading the latest news of the stock market; one lives as if one always 'might miss out on something.'"[36] For Nietzsche, this way of being is paradigmatic of the having mode, where one "lives in a constant chase after gains . . . to the point of exhaustion."[37] This inability or reluctance to be quiet and still suggests that "our civilization is turning into a new barbarism," where "time for thinking and quietness for thinking are lacking."[38] But it is not the accumulated stress, the possibility of burnout, or even the boredom of the having mode that troubles Nietzsche. It is the self-deception, the dishonesty. It is the lie grounded in an imperative that says: "One should do anything rather than nothing."[39] But old age opens up a freeing space of quietude where we can begin to let go of these conditioned habits, where we can confront the nothing and, "in the blink of an eye, in the tiniest atom of our lives, we may encounter something holy."[40]

In *Thus Spoke Zarathustra*, Nietzsche expands on this experience of the holy, reminding his readers of how important it is to walk away from the buzzing din of the market place, to "flee into your solitude ... to be like the tree that you love with its wide branches: silently listening."[41] Here he offers his own account of happiness, one that has little to do with superficial pleasures or the distracted merrymaking of the herd. In an aphorism titled "At Noon," he describes Zarathustra alone resting under the sun in a grassy meadow. "He laid on the ground in stillness and secrecy," he did nothing but listen and pay attention, and realized that this was not boredom; it was happiness.

> O happiness! O happiness! Would you sing, O my soul? You are lying in the grass. But this is the secret solemn hour when no shepherd plays his pipe. Refrain! How little is sufficient for happiness! ... Precisely the least, the softest, the lightest, a lizard's rustling, a breath, a breeze, a moment's glance—it is *little* that makes the best happiness. Still.[42]

Zarathustra here is not reflexively turning away from the nothing; he is turning toward it. He is not craving diversions or clinging to things. He is renouncing the acquisitive mode altogether and moving into the domain of being. In the stillness, he is free, released from the distractions of the marketplace and the restless grip of busyness. It is an experience of joy. "Still! Still! Did not the world become perfect just now?"[43]

Before he descended into madness, Nietzsche spent his final summers in the breathtaking mountain region of Sils Maria, Switzerland, where he rented a simple room in a modest two-storey house. He would spend long afternoons walking alone through lush forests and meadows and along the shores of Lake Sils. He referred to the area as the "breeding ground for his ideas," and to his friends he wrote: "Here my muses live."[44] He wrote his greatest works, including *Zarathustra*, in the midst of this alpine solitude, and it was the stillness of the setting that inspired his account of happiness and opened him up to the liberating mystery of the nothing. In honor of this holy place, he wrote the Buddhist-tinged poem "Sils Maria."

> Here I sat waiting, waiting—yet for nothing
> beyond good and evil, sometimes enjoying light,
> sometimes enjoying shadow, completely only play,
> completely lake, completely noon,
> completely time without goal.[45]

The poem is a renunciation of the toxic busyness of modern culture and points to the simple wisdom that can come to us in our later years. Released from the harried rush of having and doing that torments us in youth and in middle age, we are finally allowed to slow down and be still, finally allowed to understand what is true, that there is nothing enduring or permanent about the human condition. All that exists is this fleeting moment, this breath. Zarathustra reminds his readers: "*This, this* is your bliss."[46]

4

The World Has Become Smaller

You are your body and nothing besides.
Friedrich Nietzsche

In the days I spent in intensive care after my heart attack, I was painfully struck by how the physicians rarely encountered me as a person. I was reduced to numerical data disclosed through various diagnostic instruments. When they entered the room, their focus was not on me but on their computer screens and the various charts and monitors on the wall. There was rarely any eye contact when they hovered over my body, and certainly no effort to understand how I was suffering and overwhelmed as my world collapsed around me. It felt like I was just a corporeal thing to them, an object of measurement, as if my failing heart was somehow separate and distinct from my existence. In medical school, these physicians were clearly not taught that the original Greek word for person is *soma*, which means body, and they were unfamiliar with one of the guiding truths of existentialism, that "we do not 'have' a body; rather, we 'are' bodily ... *we are somebody that is alive.*"[1] The impersonal treatment I received in the hospital was in large part the byproduct of a dualistic assumption that modern medicine inherits, roughly speaking, from the French philosopher René Descartes (1596–1650), according to which the human being is composed of two substances: an immaterial mind (*res cogitans*, a thing that thinks) and a physical body (*res extensa*, a thing that has extension). On this view, the primary role of the physician is to diagnose and treat the physical body, paying little attention to how these diagnoses and treatments affect a person's psychological and emotional well-being. This is because the person and the body are regarded as two distinct substances, and the mechanical interventions carried out on the body are somehow external and ancillary to the person. The existentialist rejects Descartes' dualistic picture and argues that the body is not a substance that we are only contingently connected to. It is who we are; it is *my body* and the panoply of experiences, feelings, and meanings that belong to me and make me who I am. As Marcel puts it, "what I feel is indissolubly linked to the fact that my body is *my body*, not just one body among others . . . Nobody who is not inside my skin can know what I feel."[2]

What was mystifying about the experience of my body prior to the heart attack is the extent to which I was unaware of it. My heart and lungs worked in the background; my arms, legs, and hands merged seamlessly into the flow of everyday life as I moved through the world, handled equipment, and engaged with others. It was as if I were living through the medium of my body without explicitly reflecting on it, that my body had its own kinesthetic wisdom, a kind of practical knowledge that manifested itself in the way I was transparently locked in and geared to the world and to the movements and actions that propelled me forward. Against the standard Cartesian account that views human action as something always accompanied by mental intentions, I rarely thought about what I was doing as I went about my day; my consciousness was already embodied and fleshly. I was what Merleau-Ponty called an "incarnate consciousness" (*conscience incarnée*), a "consciousness that in the first place is not a matter of '*I think that*' but of '*I can*.'"[3] But, after my heart attack, the smooth and effortless "I can" was replaced with a debilitating "I can't." The light and fluid bond between body and world that I had long taken for granted broke down. The world no longer presented itself as an expansive horizon of projects that solicited my action, and the setting of my life began to shrink and collapse back on itself.

This phenomenon of spatial contraction reveals something unique about the human condition. We don't take up space or occupy it, like a chair or a table. Our embodied, sensory–motor capacities constitute space, they create and open up an experiential field through which we can handle things and engage with them. Understood this way, my body does not end at the skin, as if I were a bounded corporeal object. It stretches beyond itself, and is everywhere in my experience of the world. It extends seamlessly into the keyboard on which I type these words; it stretches to the trees and the lawn outside my office window; it reaches toward the sun and clouds in the distance. The unique way in which my body is already involved and caught up in the midst of things makes it impossible for me to distinguish the world from *my experience* of the world. There is no separation because human existence is, in Merleau-Ponty's words, a "closely woven fabric," and it is this tacit weave that orients and positions me in the world.[4] It allows me to perceive things in terms of directionality and proximity—of left and right, front and behind, close by and far away. And it also sustains the background sense of "I can" that keeps my experience of space open and expansive. I experience the stairs as climbable, the path as walkable, the slope as skiable.

But this unacknowledged bond inevitably frays as we get older. The powers of seeing and hearing begin to diminish, and spatially constituting activities like walking and driving become more difficult. As this occurs, the space of our lives begins to shrink, and we increasingly see ourselves as helpless and dependent objects, no longer "making space" but simply taking up space as a corporeal thing. In this way, the aging body is no longer inconspicuous; it doesn't recede into the background, as it did when we were younger. And as this transparency is disrupted, we become increasingly aware that we "have" a body; we feel the pain in our knees and our backs; we experience the limits of our eyesight and hearing; we anticipate what our stomachs can handle when we sit down for dinner at the restaurant. The body begins to emerge out of its hiddenness to reveal itself as an object, as something strange and foreign to us. But we not only feel the body as object in the various pains and discomforts that present themselves, we also see this unfamiliar thing staring back at us in the mirror in the sagging skin, the wrinkles, the dimmed eyes, the yellowed teeth and thinning hair. And we begin to notice how others look at us too.

The World Has Become Smaller

Of all the existentialists, it is Beauvoir who offers the most personal and unflinching account of this experience of alienation. In the second volume of her autobiography *The Force of Circumstance*, a fifty-five-year-old Beauvoir describes her own experience of growing old as one of spatial contraction. "The world around me has changed," she writes, "it has become smaller and narrower." She realizes that to "grow old is to set limits on oneself, to shrink," and as the world diminishes and contracts, so too does the effortless "I can" and the projects, adventures, and playfulness that gave life its spontaneous meaning and joy.[5]

> The mountain paths disdain my feet. Never again shall I collapse, drunk with fatigue, into the smell of hay. Never again shall I slide down through the solitary morning snows. Never again a man. Now, not my body alone but my imagination has accepted that. In spite of everything, *it's strange not to be a body any more.*[6]

Beauvoir goes on to explore how older adults are often complicit in the narrowing of their world by over-emphasizing their disabilities. She introduces the French psychiatric term *gribouillisme*, which captures the way older persons "plunge into old age," expressing their despair and frustration with bodily diminishment by exaggerating the severity of their own disability.

> Because he is rather lame, he goes through the motions of paralysis; because he is rather deaf, he stops listening altogether. The functions that are no longer exercised degenerate, and by playing the cripple, the subject becomes one. It is a widely spread reaction since many old people are justifiably resentful and demanding

because they have lost hope. They take revenge on the outside world by exaggerating their infirmity.[7]

In Beauvoir's eyes, this exaggerated response is understandable. When our tacit bond with the world deteriorates, the body begins to reveal itself as a clumsy and frail object, and we fall into despair seeing what the future holds for us, realizing that we are no longer able to stretch into the world with freedom and ease. "The level of inimicality in things rises," she writes, "stairs are harder to climb, distances longer to cover, streets more dangerous to cross, parcels heavier to carry. The world is filled with traps; it bristles with threats. The old person may no longer stroll casually about in it."[8] Beauvoir sees how this inimicality begins to strip away the possibilities for transcendence and the passion and commitment we had for our former projects. Bodily fatigue and the decays of aging "brings with it the impossibility of surpassing oneself and of becoming passionately concerned with anything; it kills all projects."[9]

In her memoir, Beauvoir describes how the strangeness of her aging body seemed to sneak up on her and take her by surprise. "One day I said to myself: 'I'm forty!' By the time I recovered from the shock of that discovery I had reached fifty. The stupor that seized me then has not left me yet."[10] With her signature honesty, she gives an account of her own horror in seeing herself as an old woman. The striking and charismatic *jeune femme* who helped transform postwar Paris into the intellectual and artistic epicenter of Europe was gone. The mirror revealed a face that had been weathered and wrecked by time, that was now "dead and mummified" in the eyes of others. "I loathe my appearance now," she writes, "the eyebrows slipping down toward the eyes, the bags underneath, the excessive fullness of the cheeks, and that air of sadness around the mouth that wrinkles always bring ... I see my face attacked by the pox of time for which there is no cure."[11] Beauvoir understands that in an ageist society, older persons are already pushed to the margins, into the category of the "other," but the situation is especially hard for women in a patriarchal society. In this case, the woman has already been socialized from an early age to be alienated from herself, to see her body as a fragile and delicate thing, an object of desire under the male gaze.

In her book *The Second Sex*, Beauvoir suggests that the young girl "becomes an object, and she sees herself as object; she discovers this new aspect of her being with surprise: it seems to her that she has been doubled; instead of coinciding with herself, she now begins to exist outside."[12] And the woman maintains her power largely by affirming her desirability, staying young and vibrant in an effort to hold on to her status as an erotic object. Beauvoir herself appears to fall prey to this pattern. She describes how her affair with the young journalist Claude Lanzmann, awakened her dormant sexual power and how this sheltered her from having to confront her age. "Lanzmann's presence," she writes, "freed me from my age. Thanks to him, a thousand things were restored to me: joys, astonishments, anxieties, laughter and the freshness of the world ... After ... the first warnings of physical decline, I leapt back enthralled into happiness."[13] But when the relationship ends, so does the age-defying power and intoxication of being desired, and she falls into despair once again. It is, of course, true that times have changed in the sixty years since Beauvoir published her memoirs, and a woman's value is no longer reduced to her ability to reproduce, offer domestic services, or elicit desire. But Beauvoir's frank account of her own experience helps us understand the extraordinary anti-aging efforts that the modern woman endures. With her wrinkle creams, Botox treatments, Restylane fillers, diet regimens, hormone replacement therapies, tummy tucks, and facelifts, she does everything she can to keep the old woman at bay. Beauvoir recognizes that, "when she grows old and ugly," she is often rendered invisible or, worse, she is "losing the place allotted to her in society: she becomes a *monstrum* that excites revulsion and even dread."[14]

However, as psychologist Mary Pipher has pointed out, invisibility in old age does not have to be wholly unpleasant. To be sure, a woman can be desired and can experience passion deep into old age, but, for some, no longer being noticed can be experienced as liberating. It can free her from social expectations about her physical appearance, about what she wears and how she behaves. Going unnoticed in her later years gives her permission to be "silly, quirky, and free to do as she pleases."[15] In her memoir *Somewhere toward the End*, ninety-one-year-old Diana Athill, praised as London's best editor in her day, confirms this point. She certainly laments the loss of her beauty and desirability, but at the same time observes a new kind of freedom, where "other things became more interesting." Art, gardening, reading, and many other pursuits emerged that gave her joy in ways that her younger "steamy girl" self could never experience.[16] And the writer Emily Fox Gordon describes a similar kind of freedom and sense of contentedness as she moves into her late sixties. "I've finally worked free of the agitation and misery of youth," she writes, "which in my case extended well into middle age."[17]

Focused as she is on the oppressive constraints of our sexist and ageist society, Beauvoir doesn't engage with the freedom of an older woman's invisibility and paints an exceedingly bleak picture of old age. For this reason, her book *The Coming of Age* has been widely panned as essentializing and reductive, prompting septuagenarian philosopher Martha Nussbaum to refer to it as "worse than preposterous ... it is an act of collaboration with social stigma and injustice."[18] But Nussbaum's critique appears to overlook the core contribution of existentialist thought, namely that old age, just like the factual givens of race, physical ability, or gender, can limit and constrain us only insofar as we choose to interpret them as limits. Beauvoir herself seems to forget this lesson, as she denies her own freedom and treats her aging body and the social judgments of others as if they were a suffocating destiny. "I have fought always not to let them label me," she admits, "but I have not been able to prevent the years from enmeshing me. I shall live for a long time in this little landscape where my life has come to rest."[19] But, as we now know, the foundational principle of existentialism is that "existence precedes essence," that we make ourselves who we are. This means that any reductive or essentializing label gains its meaning from us; it affects us only to the extent that we choose to yield to it.[20] And there are many ways in which we can resist ageist stereotypes and interpret our bodily diminishments positively and life-affirmingly.

Sharon Olds, the great existential poet of the body, published *Odes* in her mid-seventies. This is a collection of rebellious elegies that, with humor and awe, celebrates the uncanny beauty of her aging body. Look at how she embraces her nursing home neck in "Ode to Wattles":

> I want to write about my wattles—oooo, I
> lust after it,
> I want to hold a mirror under my
> chin so I can see the new
> events . . .
> I love to be a little disgusting,
> to go as far as I can
> into the thrilling unloveliness.[21]

Unlike Beauvoir, Olds refuses to internalize the stigmatizing judgments of society. In "Ode to Stretchmarks," she chooses to see her torn dermis not as an unsightly reminder of bodily decrepitude but as a marker of thanks for a long and rich life, one that allowed her to become who she is.

> the gleaming ripples in the silk . . .
> so the language of aging,
> the code of it, the etching, and the scribbling
> and silvering, are signs, to me, of
> getting to live out my full term,
> enduring to become what I have loved.[22]

In her memoir, Beauvoir despairs at her lost beauty and diminished physicality as inescapable reminders of death. "My powers of revolt," she laments, "are dimmed now by the imminence of my end . . . My joys have paled as well. Death is no longer a brutal event in the distance, it haunts my sleep. Awake, I sense its shadow between the world and me: it has already begun."[23] But in her poems, Olds isn't recoiling from the nearness of death evident in her failing body. She recognizes and accepts the basic truth of the human condition, that life and death are interdependent; they exist simultaneously, and if you are to celebrate the one you have to celebrate the other. In "Ode of Withered Cleavage," she writes:

> I want to live to an age when I look
> hardly human, I want to love them
> equally, birth and its daughter and
> mother, death.[24]

What is interesting is that Beauvoir herself seems to undergo a transformation as she grows older and appears to confirm the so-called paradox of well-being, according to which the pattern of happiness in life is often U-shaped: it dips in mid-life but then increases as we move into our later years. Ten years after her dreary account of turning fifty, Beauvoir is less consumed with death, bodily diminishment, and vanishing possibilities for adventure and romance. In the third and final volume of her autobiography, *All Said and Done*, she is more serene and accepting of old age. Now in her mid-sixties, she confesses: "I was mistaken . . . in the outline of my future. I had projected the accumulated disgust of the recent years into it. It has been far less somber than I had foreseen."[25] *La vieille* finds herself in the midst of a community of loving friends and is actively engaged in meaningful work. She, of course, remains unflinching in the way she documents the myriad pains, humiliations, and losses of old age, but her life as a writer and intellectual is still vibrant and rich, and her commitment to issues of oppression and social justice is unwavering. In her case, she realizes, "there is only one solution if old age is not to be a derisory parody of our former existence, and that is to go on pursuing ends that gave our life meaning—devotion to individuals, to collectives, to causes, social, political, intellectual or creative work."[26]

On this point, Martha Nussbaum counters that Beauvoir seems to be suggesting that only exceptional individuals, artists, poets, and thinkers can lead rich and meaningful lives in old age, because they have the financial means, creative gifts, and cognitive wherewithal to continue working on intellectual and artistic projects. There is certainly truth to Nussbaum's criticism, and Beauvoir herself was acutely aware of her own privilege. In *The Force of Circumstance*, she makes this clear. "Economically," she writes, "I belong to a privileged class," and this privilege was an accident; it was not something she earned. She goes on to admit: "I am a profiteer primarily because of the education I received and the possibilities it opened for me."[27] Money, beauty, bourgeois connections, and an advanced degree from the Sorbonne certainly opened doors for the young Beauvoir and provided her with a measure of recognition and access to meaningful projects in her later years. But what about those who grow old and frail in the grinding prison of poverty? Beauvoir was deeply concerned about this, and *The Coming of Age* is, in many ways, a scathing critique of the dehumanizing cruelty of contemporary capitalism, where the old and poor "are condemned to stagnate in boredom and loneliness, a mere throw-out."[28] She envisions a radical transformation of the structures of capitalism. This is an economic system where the elderly are viewed as "throw-outs" because they can no longer be exploited for profit. For

Beauvoir, to change this system would be nothing less than to "change life itself."[29] And if this were to happen, perhaps we would begin to see the elderly "as human beings, with human life behind them, and not as so many walking corpses." That would be an "obvious truth," and it "would move us profoundly."[30]

In the evening of her own life, Beauvoir recognized that, in order to live with a sense of urgency and purpose, one does not have to be famous, wealthy, or beautiful. In her prime, she was all of these things. What mattered, for her, was that she continued to care about her life and the lives of others and worked toward building a community that would be more compassionate and just. It is certainly clear in her later writings that Beauvoir was less focused on the classic existentialist themes that she and Sartre pioneered in the 1940s and 1950s—those of freedom and the self-actualizing power of the individual—and turned her attention more explicitly to the ways in which social and cultural forces limit and constrain our capacities for transcendence. In this regard, *The Coming of Age* is a testament to how older persons are stripped of their subjectivity, dehumanized, and discarded and to how they tend to internalize this image and define themselves by it in ageist societies. But Beauvoir maintains that this is not a destiny; freedom and transcendence, although they are exceedingly difficult in our current situation, are still possible. "There is nothing," she writes, "that obliges us in our hearts to recognize ourselves in the frightening image that others provide us with. That is why it is possible to reject that image verbally and refuse it by means of our behavior."[31]

It is, of course, true that the world contracts as we grow older, as society turns its back on us, and as our sensory–motor capacities diminish. But we now see that, in the wake of this diminishment, other aspects of our existence come alive. In the last months of his life, the octogenarian neurologist and author Oliver Sacks reflected on this curious aspect of transcendence. He was by then slow and small in the wake of metastatic cancer, yet he noticed "not a shrinking but an enlargement of mental life and perspective." He observed that he was more "conscious of transience and, perhaps, of beauty," and described a new experience of freedom beginning to emerge.[32] But it was one that had nothing to do with the acquisitive, ego-driven desires of his younger days. Indeed, it was freedom *from* those very desires that he found so gratifying. The great world traveler and writer who swam a mile a day into his eighties was now bedridden, reduced to a weakened shell of his former self. But in the midst of this fleshly decay, he referred to feeling "intensely alive."[33] Sacks' words convey a forceful sense of agency, a refusal to see himself as a walking corpse, as a being condemned to the facticity of his body. In true existentialist fashion, he describes how cancer and ageist stereotypes don't define him and shows that there is no pre-given essence that determines who he is, that he is a self-creating being right up until the end. This is why, he says, it is ultimately "*up to me* how to choose to live out the months that remain," and it is up to each one of us "to find his own path, to live his own life," and "to die his own death."[34]

5

Be the Poet of Your Life

Man is always a storyteller . . . and he tries to live his life as if to tell it.

Jean-Paul Sartre

As we have seen, one of the enduring contributions of existentialism is the recognition that the self is not a static thing or substance. It is an interpretive activity, an ongoing process of self-creation, and we exist in the meanings that we create for ourselves, that we care about, and that are made available by the situation we've been thrown into. This is why Nietzsche says that "existence without interpretation . . . is precisely nonsense."[1] We fashion ourselves by telling a story about who we are and what matters in our lives, and our identities are held together by its narrative unity and cohesion. In the absence of this story-like structure, our sense of who we are would be confused, fragmented, and disjointed. But our stories are not told in a vacuum. They are always dependent on and bound up with the world; they exist in a wider context of shared meanings, languages, cultural institutions, and practices that we

69

ourselves did not create.[2] Nietzsche refers to this view as "perspectivism" (*Perspektivismus*), which postulates that there are no timeless, transhistorical truths; there are only historically mediated perspectives or interpretations, and our story-shaped selves are so embedded in these interpretative contexts that "we cannot see around our own corner."[3] This means that the process of narrative self-fashioning is always social or "dialogical." It takes place against a background of past experiences and cultural meanings that are laid out in advance and that we continually adopt and appropriate as our lives unfold.[4] But this view of the self presents unique challenges for older persons.

The first challenge is the problem of memory loss as we age. One of the assumptions built into the narrative conception of the self is that we have a relatively cohesive sense of our past; this sense is guaranteed by a recollective capacity that allows us to identify the significant events in our lives. But the forgetfulness that accompanies old age undermines this capacity and disrupts the unity and cohesion of our story; and this can be terrifying. Struggling with the loss of his own memory in his later years, Irvin Yalom admits: "Losing so much of my life when I am still alive—that is truly frightening."[5] But Nietzsche reminds us that these "senior moments" are not all bad. They often allow us to forget the painful missteps, slights, and transgressions that come with a long life. Indeed, the inability to remember can be viewed as a source of healing, even strength. Thus Nietzsche writes in *On the Genealogy of Morals*:

> To be incapable of taking one's enemies, one's accidents, even one's *misdeeds* seriously for very long—such is the

sign of strong full natures, natures in possession of a surplus of the power to shape, form, and heal, of the power which also enables one to forget (a good example of this in the modern world is Mirabeau, who had no memory for the insults and malicious behavior directed against him and could not forgive simply because he could not—remember). Such a man with a single shrug shakes off much of that which worms and digs its way into others.[6]

When we are young, the sting of the past, of guilt, regret, and *ressentiment* can torment us. But failing to remember is not a sign of weakness or failure. For Nietzsche, there is a kind of nobility in selective forgetting, because "*ressentiment* simply fails to appear."[7] And recent studies on aging and cognition have shown that this selective capacity that older persons display may make it easier for them to recall and focus on pleasurable memories and to forget those that are painful.[8]

A related challenge to the idea of the story-shaped self is the assumption that our story is heading somewhere, that it has a teleological nature and is moving inexorably toward its completion. Old age, on this reading, is an apex or culmination, the point at which we can look back on our life and grasp its narrative unity.[9] Of course, the gaps in memory that come in later years undermine this view. An even more serious threat is dementia, where memory, language, and higher-order cognition become so impaired that the very possibility of selfhood can be called into question. So, if we adopt the teleological assumption, can the human being still be called a "self" or a "person" in the late stages of Alzheimer's disease, when one is no longer able to tell one's story, to interpret and give meaning to one's life, and to integrate the disjointed events of the past into a meaningful and coherent pattern? As Heidegger reminds us, it is this meaning-giving capacity that distinguishes us as humans; without it we cease to exist as such. "It is not just one possible comportment (among others)," he writes. "It is the basis of our existence," it "*constitutes selfhood.*"[10]

On what may be considered a hard reading of existentialism, the property of selfhood would not be attributed to those who lack agency or the capacity to take responsibility for their lives.[11] But this reading is overly narrow and restrictive, if agency is reduced to mental activity located inside the mind or brain. As we saw in the previous chapter, the existentialist forwards the idea of an embodied and embedded self, one that is already involved in the world, bound up with it. It is a self that is expressed not just in detached cognition, but in our embodied movement and orientation, in the pre-reflective handling of tools, in interpersonal gestures and tactile interactions with others. It is, of course, true that Alzheimer's profoundly disrupts higher-order cognition, speech, and memory, and it certainly undermines the ability to lead a life and fashion a coherent narrative. But this does not mean that it completely strips away the dignity of selfhood. Even in cases of severe dementia, the individual is still aware, receptive, and open to the world on the basis of a "body schema" (*schéma corporel*), as Merleau-Ponty calls it: an embodied system of sensory–motor capacities that "radiates from us to our environment."[12] The Alzheimer's patient can still reach out, handle, and touch things, and be aroused by the solicitations of the world, by a melody, an old photograph, or a familiar voice, by watching birds out the window, by feeling the warmth of a blanket or the gentle touch of another person. Indeed, with the proper care and support, the individual can continue to have experiences that are significant and pleasurable.

The point of this is not to dismiss the despair and confusion that comes with dementia but to add a layer of complexity to the question of what it means "to be" a self. All too often Alzheimer's sufferers are cast into a liminal state of being not quite human, on account of deteriorations in memory and cognition. But, as Nietzsche reminds us, there is something deeper and more primordial to who we are than our cognitive capacities; "behind your thoughts . . . stands a mighty ruler, an unknown sage—whose name is self. In your body he dwells, *he is your body.*"[13] If caregivers can tap into this bodily wisdom, they can be witness to moments of freely expressed affection, joy, even lucidity. In a memoir that documents the care offered to her own afflicted husband, Marie Marley gives a moving account of these tender joys and even suggests that the fear, denial, and depression might be more painful for family members and caregivers than it is for the sufferer.[14] Irvin Yalom brings this point to light when he confronts his own fear of visiting his beloved mentor from medical school, the well-known psychiatrist Jerome Frank—who at the time lived in a residential facility and suffered from severe dementia. When he asked Frank what his present life was like, Yalom was consoled by Frank's equanimous response. "Every day is a new day," came the answer, "I wake up and whoosh . . . Yesterday's all gone. But I sit in this chair and watch life go by. It's not so bad, Irv. It's not so bad."[15]

Putting aside the moral implications of what counts as a person, the more pressing challenge to the idea of the story-shaped self is the fact that the discursive material required for composing one's narrative is largely ageist. Media images and popular culture depict old age as a time of decline, despair, and dependency. These depictions are often internalized, which leads to a situation where older persons oppress themselves by trying to deny or avoid the aging process altogether or allow themselves to suffer from anxiety and diminished self-esteem because they can't bear who they are becoming.[16] They are bombarded with youth-obsessed messages that portray older persons as useless, unattractive, and frail. Hence the available resources that can support edifying ways of narratively reframing later life are limited. And, if this is our present situation, what are the implications for selfhood? If a basic condition of being human is that we understand and make sense of who we are in the form of a narrative, then how can older persons combat these dehumanizing stereotypes and craft a satisfying and meaningful story in their final years?[17]

This is a difficult question, and it helps us understand Beauvoir's claim, in *The Coming of Age*, that self-awareness about growing old is often not a gradual or progressive experience. It tends to creep up on us and to take us by surprise, and "when it seizes upon our own personal life, we are dumbfounded."[18] Enculturated as we are by ageist prejudices, we see old age as a kind of boundary that, once crossed, cuts us off from who we previously were. Often after a significant milestone or life event—retirement, loss of a loved one, critical illness—we suddenly experience ourselves, in Beauvoir's words, "as something alien, a foreign species."[19] When this happens, the unity and coherence of our story is disrupted, because the future no longer opens up a space of meaningful possibilities that we can project for ourselves. To Beauvoir, this explains the unique relationship older persons have with time. "They refuse time because they do not wish to decline; they define their former I as that which they still are—they assert solidarity with their youth."[20] But clinging to the past in this way is an expression of bad faith; it is self-deceptive because it denies the structural futurity (or forward-directedness) of existence and assumes the reality of a former identity that is somehow immutable and secure. "They set up a fixed, unchanging essence against the deteriorations of age, and tirelessly they tell stories of this being that they were, this being that lives on inside them."[21]

This denial in old age is understandable because, in our society, the future reveals itself largely as a time of disappointment and decline. Today we generally interpret growing old in one of two ways. We can "age poorly" and passively succumb to a period of relentless deterioration; or we can "age well" and work to stay young and vital for as long as possible.[22] But neither of these narratives provides an honest picture of the unique value, pleasure, and perspective that emerge in later life.[23] And the existentialist understands that these constrictive narratives don't represent a destiny, that older persons don't have to give in and conform to these culturally sanctioned expectations. He or she always has the power to rebel, that is, to say "No!"

Albert Camus famously describes the rebel as someone who says "no and yes simultaneously."[24] The rebel says "No!" to our ageist culture and its dehumanizing stereotypes, experiencing it with a "feeling of revulsion

at the infringement of his rights." But at the same time
the rebel says "Yes!" to life and the self-fashioning story
he or she tells and, in this way, embodies "a complete
and spontaneous loyalty to" him- or herself.[25] As an
incarnation of rebellion, the older person remains loyal
or true to him- or herself by refusing to tell his or her
story within the narrative constraints of ageism. And,
for Camus, these acts of rebellion transcend individual
interests by demonstrating solidarity with other elders
who are abject and suffer under similar conditions. This
is why "an act of rebellion is not, essentially an egoistic
act . . . The rebel demands respect for himself, of course,
but only insofar as he identifies himself with a natural
community." In this way the rebel takes a stand on
ageism by illuminating our shared humanity and the
imperative of preserving a sense of meaning and dignity
in the latter stages of life; he or she is "revealing the part
of man which must be defended."[26] Rebellion, then, is
the way we rise above, or surpass, the forces that limit
and constrain us; and, for Camus, this process is nothing less than the bursting forth of life itself. Rebellion
is fundamental to being human. As an expression of
transcendence, this act "gives birth to existence" and
creates fellowship in the face of shared suffering. This is
how Camus comes to reformulate the famous Cartesian
dictum, from "I *think*, therefore I am" to "I *rebel*,
therefore I am."[27] But what does this mean for our
story-shaped selves? Rebellion is a crucial starting point,
but it is certainly not enough. We still need to find the
material to craft a meaningful conclusion to our lives.
But if the only narratives our culture offers us are those
of inescapable decline on the one hand and age-denying
desperation on the other, what can we turn to?

Here again, the existentialists provide insight by questioning our hardened tendency to conform to the ready-made norms and expectations of the public world. They warn that, when we drift along with the crowd in this way, we are disburdened from having to own up to the givens of our condition or from taking responsibility for the course of our lives. Heidegger develops this idea in *Being and Time*, where he suggests that this everyday way of existing is "tranquilizing" (*beruhigend*) for us; it creates the comforting illusion that we are living a good life because we are doing what "they" do. But this "they," for Heidegger, does not simply represent the attitude of everydayness. It is also the source of *all* our interpretive meanings; it is "the referential context of significance" itself.[28] In consequence, this category, "they," provides the resources that make it possible for us to tell our story. This makes it difficult to challenge the youth-obsessed perspective that dominates today. It opens up a very narrow and constricted range of possibilities and simultaneously conceals other narrative meanings and ways of living. When we are caught up in everydayness, we conform to the expectations of this constricted perspective, and this prevents us from accessing what Heidegger calls our "heritage" (*Erbeschaft*)—a reference to "former ways of revealing" that have been covered over and forgotten in the harried and disjointed bustle of modern life.[29] One of the aims of Heidegger's project, then, is to develop a deep historical awareness of who we are, so that we may recover older interpretative resources that lie beneath the crust of our current self-understanding. This is why he says that "to understand history cannot mean anything else than to understand ourselves."[30] And, temporally, this suggests that our existence does not stretch just forward, into the future; it also stretches backward, into the past, toward our historical beginnings.[31]

In this task of historical recovery we can identify powerful counternarratives, which challenge our ageist worldview and provide rich material we can draw on to help fashion a meaningful story in the late stages of life. The American philosopher Drew Leder offers up a number of possibilities. There is the path of *the contemplative*, for example, which sees retirement, the empty house, and even the declining body not as a loss but an opportunity to slow down and reflect on the meaning of life. This is a narrative that interprets old age as a time of solitude and spiritual development, a time for study, prayer, and meditation, or simply a time of communing with nature. There is also the path of *the contributor*, who experiences elderhood as a time of passing on the wisdom and lessons of a long life and freely mentoring younger folk willing to receive this wisdom. Here older adults might fashion their later years through mentoring programs for children at risk or in foster care; they would participate in local tutoring and enrichment experiences or devote themselves to difficult social problems or environmental causes. There is also the path of *the compassionate companion*, where elders might draw on the historical archetypes of Christ or the Buddha as well as on their own experiences of debilitation, pain, and loss in old age to offer comfort and care to those who are suffering alone in hospices, homeless shelters, or long-term care facilities. And there is finally the path of *the creative*, who rejects the idea that older adults are inflexible and stuck in their ways. Creative elders do not wallow in the past but narrate a life that is open and receptive to new ways of being. They see old age as a time of reinvention, a time to be curious, to take up painting, poetry, or tai chi; they might move to a new part of town, join a community theater, or even reacquaint themselves with the philosophy of existentialism in order to help them confront old age and death.[32]

Whichever path we choose to craft our narrative in later life, the existentialist makes it clear that our story will always be unfinished. Human existence is never complete; it is an activity, a state of becoming, always unfolding and open-ended. As Nietzsche writes, "[b]ecoming must be explained without recourse to final intentions ... Becoming does not aim at a final state ... does not flow into 'being.'"[33] This means that there can be no tidy end or conclusion to our story so long as we are alive, self-aware, and capable of making choices about who we are. I am a "not yet," always in the process of making myself who I am, but this process of self-making is always vulnerable; it can break down and collapse at certain points in our life. Much like the heart attack that shattered the narrative I had of myself as a healthy and athletic college professor, the awareness of oneself as crossing into old age is often experienced as just this kind of breakdown, where we find it difficult to make sense of ourselves and our place in the world. But, for the existentialist, this crisis creates an opportunity for renewal and transformation by exposing prevailing views not as enduring truths but as fleeting historical constructs. And, in the midst of the collapse, new meanings and ways of living that had been concealed can be brought forth and illuminated, meanings that we can project for ourselves in drafting the final chapter of our story. Heidegger describes the way we take over and appropriate these new meanings in times of crisis as "poetizing" (*Dichten*) or "projective saying" (*entwerfende Sagen*), a form of narrative self-fashioning that "brings the unsayable [*Unsagbare*] as such into the world."[34] In this way, a future previously darkened by ageist discrimination and prejudice is lit up again with interpretative possibilities that were previously inconceivable. The crisis temporarily frees us and opens us up to ways of being that may allow us to engage with what is genuinely meaningful and worthwhile about growing old. It allows us to envision the type of person we want to be at the end of our lives, project that vision forward, and try to bring it into some form of realization.[35]

But these narrative possibilities are not projected *ex nihilo*, as if old age offers us a clean slate for self-creation. As the American philosopher Alexander Nehamas suggests in his pioneering interpretation of Nietzsche, if the story of my life is to have any measure of intelligibility and cohesion, I have to try to gather together and integrate the past and all that I have done, because those experiences are decisive in shaping who I am today.[36] For Nehamas, the act of consolidating the disparate threads of one's life into a unified whole is what Nietzsche means when he says: "You must become who you are."[37] Nietzsche understands that existence is never static; it is a "mulitiplicity ... the continual transitoriness and fleetingness of the subject,"[38] and this often results in a life that is scattered and disjointed, pulled apart by a haphazard tangle of character traits, experiences, desires, and conditioned habits. Against this fragmented backdrop, we become who we are by storyizing our lives, embracing these muddled attributes, and integrating them into a cohesive and organized narrative. Nietzsche calls this "giving style" to one's character.

> It is practiced by those who survey all the strengths and weaknesses of their nature and then fit them into an artistic plan until every one of them appears as art and reason and even weaknesses delight the eye. Here a large mass of second nature has been added; there a piece of original nature has been removed—both times through long practice and daily work at it.[39]

And, for Nietzsche, crafting this artistic plan and giving style to existence is not a young person's game; it is a "long practice," one that takes time and patience as we gather together the painful and poignant lessons of our lives. As Zarathustra says, "Verily, I too have learned to wait—thoroughly—but only to wait for *myself*."[40] It is only in the act of creating oneself out of everything that has happened that one can truly "*learn* to love oneself."[41] This generally means that the young are not yet artists, because they cling too rigidly to the false security of "the unconditional" (*das Unbedingte*) and are unable to accept and integrate the unsettling forces of contingency, nuance, and multiplicity that shape them. There is, then, a kind of inflexibility and ignorance when we are young, "something falsifying and deceptive" about who we think we are.[42] The suggestion is that, as we grow older, we become more flexible, more comfortable with change and ambiguity, and this deepens and broadens our sense of who we are, allowing us to affirm the unstable reality of becoming, the ceaseless process of integration and interpretation that is nothing less than existence itself. To become who one is, then, is not to reach an end state; this is not the finale at which becoming stops. It is rather an act of affirming and embracing the terrible and wondrous event of becoming, and working to fit it all into a coherent and artistic plan.

This appears to be what Nietzsche means when he says: "we want to be the poets of our life." To live poetically is to "make things beautiful, attractive, and desirable even when they are not."[43] And this may be one of the most liberating gifts of growing old; old age brings its own wisdom, "an affirmation of the world *as it is*, without subtraction, exception, or selection."[44] Jonas Mekas, the ninety-two-year-old survivor of the Nazi concentration camps to whom we were introduced earlier, appeared to be the embodiment of this Nietzschean formula. He was wholly accepting of all that had come before him; he understood that the entirety of disjointed traits, acts, and traumas served as the narrative material for his life; and he was somehow able to take to this material, organize it, and, like a poet, transform it into a cohesive and unified work of art. In the last years of his life he gave a reading from an unpublished novella at a Greenwich Village jazz club called the Zinc Bar. When he took the stage, he looked at the audience of students, artists, and friends—an audience that spanned four generations. He began with an expression of simple astonishment: "Have you ever thought about how amazing, really amazing, life is?"[45] These words captured the sense that everything he had done and all the horrible and beautiful things he had witnessed and experienced had led him to that stage on that Sunday afternoon, that he would not want his life to be any different from what it is, and that he would be willing to live this same life again and again. Zarathustra puts it well: "'Was *that* life?' I want to say to death. 'Well then! Once more!'"[46]

6

The World in All Its Terror

Life is at the start a chaos in which one is lost.
José Ortega y Gasset

For me, it was the evenings in the intensive care unit that were the most difficult. The social buzz in the hallways would quieten down, visitors would leave, the lights would dim, and I would be left alone to confront my perilous situation. I remember an especially vivid dream one night: I found myself abandoned in a dark room, strapped to a hospital bed and unable to move, my legs in a state of forced extension to keep the intravenous medication flowing. In the dream I began to panic, thrashing out, pulling at the IV tubes, and gasping in the inky blackness. I woke up soaking wet and shaking, relieved that it was only a dream. But as my eyes adjusted to my surroundings, I quickly realized I was alone in the dark, immobile, strapped to a hospital bed. A desperate feeling of loneliness washed over me, and it was terrifying. For the existentialist, this terror emerges when we run up against a basic truth of the human condition: we are all, ultimately,

84

alone and helpless in the face of a cold and indifferent universe.

Drawing on insights from Kierkegaard and Heidegger, the German psychoanalyst Erich Fromm offers an account of this basic experience:

> The awareness of our aloneness and separateness, of our helplessness before the forces of nature and of society, all this makes our separate, disunited existence an unbearable prison. The experience of separateness arouses anxiety; it is indeed the source of all anxiety. Being separate means being cut off, without any capacity to use my human powers. Hence to be separate means to be helpless, unable to grasp the world—things and people—actively; it means that the world can invade me without my ability to react.[1]

Fromm's words capture my experience that the world's indifference had "invaded me"; and they cut to the core of who we are. Regardless of how rich our social lives are, how integrated we are into our communities, or how confident and assured we are in our identities, there is, lurking in the background, an unsettling sense of our own aloneness. But here it is important to distinguish fundamental (or existential) loneliness from more common experiences. We can, of course, feel lonely when we move to a new city, when a friendship or a marriage ends, when parents die, or when we struggle with social skills that others take for granted. And we can also feel alone in the midst of wider cultural shifts that cause the loss of social institutions that used to foster intimacy and fellowship—for instance the loss of the extended family, the church, the neighborhood bookstore or coffee shop, or the trusted family doctor.[2]

This sense of disconnection has reached such epidemic proportions today that in 2016 British Prime Minister Theresa May created a new administrative role with an Orwellian title: minister of loneliness.

Assigned to fill the role of minister of loneliness was the British Conservative politician Tracey Crouch. As a member of parliament, Crouch spoke of being blessed with a "network of friends, family, and a wonderful partner," but she also described deep feelings of alienation, of being cut off from the world, which led to a depression that lasted for six years. She was, in her own words, "in a very dark place, a very lonely place."[3] For the existentialist, what Crouch portrayed here is not a transient or situational feeling directed at a specific circumstance or life event, although she attributed her sense of estrangement largely to the breakdown of community and the isolating features of a life increasingly mediated by screens and impersonal texts and tweets from our smartphones. What she referred to is something more diffused and atmospheric, an experience that transcends the alienation of the present age. It is a sense of forlornness or abandonment that belongs to human existence itself. Heidegger called this enveloping mood "the uncanny" (*das Unheimliche*), and the German word is helpful if we want to understand the experience. Related to the word "home" (*Heim*), *heimlich* conveys a sense of being familiar and intimate. We embody this ambient feeling of being at home when things are running smoothly, when we feel that we belong and are "secure" and "cozy" (*heimelig*) in our everyday habits. By contrast, being or feeling *unheimlich* emerges when the homey façade collapses and things begin to reveal themselves as eerie and unsettled. And this illuminates a deeper, second meaning of *unheimlich*, which relates to a secret that has been exposed. The secret, in this case, is that the familiarity we take for granted is fundamentally insecure and unstable, that our existence is groundless; it rests on *nothing*.[4] For the existentialist, then, Crouch's experience of loneliness discloses a basic truth about the human condition: that we have never been at home in the world, that we are radically alone.

The experience of our essential aloneness invariably presses in on us as we grow older. As we retire from work, as our friends, relatives, and spouses die, as ageist norms push us further into the margins of everydayness, we come to be cut off from webs of social connection that give our lives a sense of stability and recognition. And the health risks of this isolation can be lethal among the elderly. Studies have shown that isolation dramatically increases rates of heart disease and stroke; it can magnify the risk of dementia and contributes to a higher incidence of depression and anxiety. Today nearly a quarter of the people over sixty-five who live independently are considered socially isolated, and nearly half of those over sixty report feeling lonely much of the time.[5] Needless to say, all this has been exacerbated by the quarantines and social distancing measures mandated by public health officials during the coronavirus pandemic. When in-person visits are prohibited in nursing homes, when senior centers, theaters, gyms, and restaurants are shuttered, older persons are especially vulnerable to the experience of the uncanny, as they become disconnected from the people, places, and projects that provided them with a sense of home, that gave their lives meaning and purpose and nourished their identities. In the forced isolation of the pandemic, the familiar hold we have on things slips away. This kind of slipping away was no doubt on Heidegger's mind when he wrote: "What is 'it' that makes one feel uncanny? . . . we can get no hold on things. In the slipping away of beings only this 'no hold on things' comes over us and remains."[6] When we lose hold of these social meanings, we become acutely aware of our own separateness. And, for older persons, this awareness can bring with it a sense of being forgotten, a feeling that no one cares or is thinking about them, that they are unloved and their lives no longer matter.

Heidegger's student, the German social philosopher Hannah Arendt, expands on this idea through her distinction between "isolation" (*Isolation*) and "loneliness" (*Verlassenheit*). Isolation occurs in "the political realm of life," a realm where a person is uprooted or cut off from the meaningful relations of the public sphere; and this makes it difficult for that person to come together and act in solidarity with others, which, for Arendt, is the source of a person's political power. This kind of experience is all too familiar to older adults, in whom isolation manifests itself in feelings of being helpless and ineffective. But in its more extreme incarnation the experience can transcend the political realm and affect one's existence as a whole.[7] It is at this point that isolation morphs into loneliness and becomes uncanny. The result is a state of being existentially homeless, an "experience of not belonging to the world at all, which is among the most radical and desperate experiences of man."[8] This state is less common in youth and middle age, when we are absorbed in the practical affairs of life, but it can be found there as well. At any rate, Arendt suggests that it can become an everyday experience for older adults.[9] Effectively removed from the world and forgotten, stored in nursing homes or residential centers, they are often deserted and rendered "superfluous."[10] This explains why the word *Verlassenheit*—which can also be translated as "abandonment" or "desertedness"—is so appropriate. It renders the experience of being discarded and alone. With no one there to acknowledge your experiences, to affirm your perceptions, or to hear your truths, your hold on the world and sense of self begins to break down. "What makes loneliness so unbearable," writes Arendt, "is the loss of one's own self . . . In this situation man loses trust in himself as the partner of his thoughts and that elementary confidence in the world which is necessary to make experiences at all. Self and world, capacity for thought and experience are lost at the same time."[11] And, as a student of existentialism, Arendt recognizes the inherent paradox of loneliness. It is "contrary to the basic requirements of the human condition," yet at the same time it is an inescapable given of our condition; it is "one of the fundamental experiences of every human life."[12] And we spend much of our time as adults in a state of self-deception or denial, trying to defend ourselves against loneliness by pretending that we are not alone.

There are many kinds of defensive strategies we employ. In our own image-obsessed culture, for example, we can receive recognition and affirmation from others by developing rich social media profiles on Instagram, Twitter, and Facebook that document our adventures and successes; and the number of "likes" we receive from each post confirms that we exist and matter in the eyes of others. According to Yalom, this is akin to a child's incessant plea to the mother: "Watch me,"

"Look at me."[13] The idea that our identity and sense of who we are are largely dependent on how others see us is foundational to existentialist thought. According to Sartre, for instance, I become aware of who I am largely through "the look" (*le regard*) of the other. I am, in this regard, "a being for others" (*un être-pour-autrui*), which means that I see myself as I do—say, as attractive, charming, successful—only insofar as others see me this way. This is why Sartre claims: I am "possessed by the Other; the Other's look fashions my body in its nakedness, causes it to be born, sculptures it, produces it as it is, sees it as I shall never see it. The Other holds a secret—*the secret of what I am*."[14] On this view I seek the attention of others because it creates the illusion that I matter and am not alone, that there is something solid, thing-like, and real about who I am. Without the other's recognition and acknowledgment, I am lost.

Another strategy in defending oneself against loneliness is to try to merge or fuse with others, to see oneself as part of another person. Here the primary orientation is one of dependence, a state in which we sacrifice our own needs and desires by conforming to the expectations of the other.[15] We find safety in this merger by turning away from the unsettling struggle for freedom and individuation, and the "I" disappears into the "we."[16] Kierkegaard is well known for examining this mode of evasion, in which we flee the anxiety of freedom for the security of being absorbed by or into the other. Often this is accomplished through institutions like marriage, where we find shelter in specious vows taken to hold "always" and "forever" and where "husband and wife promise to love one another for eternity ... and are said to become one."[17] The same

90

mode can also show up in sexual obsessiveness and compulsivity, as our promiscuous "coupling" provides a temporary reprieve from our loneliness.[18] Kierkegaard famously explores this strategy with the young hedonist Johannes in his *Diary of a Seducer*. Johannes lives for moments of sensual pleasure, hoping to turn each sexual exploit into a refuge where the "instant of enjoyment" becomes "a little eternity," which protects him from loneliness.[19] When the rush of seduction wears off with one woman, he simply moves on to the next one, with no guilt or regret. He writes: "The time is soon; always my soul requires rejuvenescence . . . Why is a young girl so pretty, and why does it last so short a time? I could become quite melancholy over this thought and yet it is no concern of mine."[20] For Johannes, women are not persons, they are abstractions, essentially indistinguishable from one another. They are to be enjoyed in the moment and discarded when the thrill of merging fades.[21]

Giving ourselves over to the idea of God can also play a central role in alleviating our aloneness. Freud refers to this experience as a kind of ego dissolution, an "oceanic feeling" (*ozeanisches Gefühl*) born out of our primordial need for protection—a need that arises, in turn, out of "the infant's helplessness and the longing for the father."[22] As we move into adolescence and adulthood, we come to the startling realization that our parents are weak and imperfect; they are not ultimate rescuers who will be there forever, to love and protect us. So we search for comfort elsewhere and lose ourselves in the sheltering arms of an all-powerful, all-loving God, a cosmic father who will always watch over us. This is why, in his critiques of Christianity, Nietzsche refers to the Gospels "as books of seduction."[23] We are tempted by the comforting illusion of a cosmic father; this illusion is "alleviating, soothing, and gratifying" to such an extent that we become "*dependent on him.*"[24] When Nietzsche's madman announces that "God is dead," he is disclosing a painful truth about the human condition. We, humans, invented the truth of God partly in order to shield ourselves from our loneliness, and then we forgot that we invented it. "Truths," as Nietzsche writes, "are illusions which we have forgotten are illusions . . . it is only by means of forgetfulness that man can reach the point of fancying himself to possess a 'truth.'"[25] And, as we slowly awaken to the reality of God's death, we become conscious of our uncanny predicament. "Aren't we now wandering as if through an endless nothing?" asks the madman. "Isn't empty space breathing upon us? Hasn't it gotten colder? Isn't night and more night continuously coming upon us? . . . How can we console ourselves?"[26]

As the world slowly abandons us in old age, the strategies we employ to defend against loneliness gradually begin to erode and break down, but the existentialist reminds us that these evasive strategies were doomed from the start. Loneliness can't be completely covered over or denied, because it is a condition of being human. And we all have a tacit sense that this is the case. As the Protestant existentialist Paul Tillich writes,

> Man is not only alone; he also knows that he is alone. Aware of what he is, he therefore asks the question of his aloneness. He asks why he is alone and how can he overcome his being alone. He cannot stand it either. It is his destiny to be alone and to be aware of it. Not even God can take away this destiny from him.[27]

On this view, the more we try to escape loneliness, the more we deny who we are; and the more we deny who we are, the more we are tormented by the anxiety of being alone.[28] To be authentic or true to ourselves, then, we should not flee from aloneness but turn toward it and try to integrate it into our lives. This act of turning toward opens us up to our predicament and allows us to perceive vulnerability and loneliness not just in ourselves but in others; and this can enrich and deepen our relationships. In fact social psychologists have shown that old age often creates this opening, which can help neutralize the pain of isolation. Older adults tend to have a heightened appreciation of their own vulnerability, and they recognize that their time is limited. As a result, they are often more willing to let go of their defenses, allowing for a more intimate, tender, and honest mode of communication with others.[29] Rather than maintaining the expansive and shallow social networks of youth and middle age, they would avoid superficial talk, preferring the deep and emotionally satisfying connections of family and close friends. And it has been found that, through this kind of selectivity of social partners, older persons are often able to maintain more positive emotions.[30]

Martin Buber puts an existentialist spin on this idea in his masterwork *I and Thou*. There he suggests that most of our adult lives are mired in an objectifying and instrumental attitude. This is what he calls the "I–it" (*Ich–Es*) relationship: a mode in which we regard the other—the cashier at the grocery store, the colleague down the hall, the racquetball partner, even a spouse or a lover—as a functional thing, an "it" to be manipulated and used for our own purposes. This relationship is comforting and stable, as it creates the illusion that we have mastery and control over things. But, for Buber, it also "erects a crucial barrier" between us: it generates feelings of loneliness by casting what he calls a "spell of separation."[31] In the "it" world there is no attempt to open up to the other, to be vulnerable and honest about our innermost fears and anxieties. As a result, that world lacks a sense of shared intimacy and connection, qualities that are essential in genuine communication. This is why Buber claims that "whoever lives only" in that world "is not human," because the attitude fails to acknowledge the other as a person, as a helpless being who is also frightened and alone, just like me.[32] There is no "sacrifice or risk" when we relate to the other as an "it."[33] We wear a mask, covering our aloneness.

Buber contrasts this with the "I–you" (*Ich–Du*) relationship, a reciprocal or mutual encounter where one withholds nothing and relates to the other with his or her whole being. It is a relation not mediated by ego-driven preconceptions of manipulation or possessiveness. In an I–you relationship "everything mediated become[s] negligible,"[34] which means that all the "it"-like defenses we cling to in order to deny our vulnerability, careers, wealth, professional titles, physical appearance, health, and fitness collapse into triviality. This is what Buber means by "the risk" (*das Risiko*): that there are no masks, no defenses, that one's whole being is involved in the I–you relation and that "whoever commits himself" in this way "may not hold back part of himself."[35] This not holding back allows the other to see me as defenseless and exposed and, ideally, this openness and vulnerability would be reciprocated. This is, for Buber, the source of all mature love; it is an experience whereby "two human beings reveal the You to one another."[36] By sharing our basic frailty and defenselessness in this way, we come to feel less alone. This is the kind of relationship that "throws a bridge from self-being to self-being across the abyss of dread."[37] As an existentialist, Buber makes it clear that there is no cure for loneliness; it is structural to the human condition, so we must confront it, even welcome it into our lives.[38] This is painful, but when I encounter the other as a "you," I enter what Buber calls an interpersonal space, "the between" (*das Zwischen*), which opens me up to a "genuine original unity," and I realize that the other is in the same predicament I am in and faces the same loneliness.[39] In these moments a bond is created and "the spell of separation broken."[40] We are consoled in this space of mutual vulnerability, because we share the experience together.

Buber's focus on the pain of loneliness was profoundly shaped by events in his own life. He confesses: "I had what the psychoanalysts would call a bad childhood."[41] Buber had a comfortable and sheltered upbringing in fin-de-siècle Vienna until the age of four, when his parents separated; he was suddenly abandoned by his mother and realized that she was never coming back. He was sent to his wealthy paternal grandparents, who raised him, but the trauma of abandonment haunted him for the rest of his life. He treated this experience as a "foretaste of death."[42]

Buber met his mother briefly thirty years later, when he was in his early thirties, but referred to the encounter as a "mismeeting" (*Vergegnung*), a term he coined to capture a situation where a person fails to interact with another in honesty and openness, in the reciprocal space of the between.[43] Yet this experience proved to be pivotal to the development of his dialogical philosophy, as it revealed to him the salvific power of the I–you encounter. Buber grew to recognize how important it is to turn your attention to the other, to put away the distractions of the cellphone, to make eye contact, and to be wholly present, because it is "only when the You becomes present" that authentic communication can take place.[44] But he also understood that these intimate encounters are intense, demanding, even dangerous, and we cannot stay in them for long. "Their spell may be seductive," he writes, "but they pull us dangerously to extremes ... shaking up our security, altogether uncanny"; if we dwell in the exposure of the I–you relationship for too long, "it would consume us."[45] But, as he grew older, Buber became more comfortable in this liminal space. When he was well into his eighties visitors would call on him, often several times a day, and he would not tolerate small talk or gossip. He wanted to *hear* the person and to have a genuine dialogue about that person's own vulnerability and loneliness. What he liked best about these encounters, wrote his friend and biographer Maurice Friedman, "was that his guest should bring him burning problems ... They should speak to him of what troubled them when they awoke in the gray of dawn and would not let them go to sleep again."[46]

In old age, as we get closer to the precipice, the hardened shell of the ego cracks open, and it may become easier to reach across the abyss and share in the experience of loneliness. This not only releases wellsprings of compassion, it can also soften our fear of abandonment and death. In a poem called "The Fiddler" written in the last months of his life, Buber describes this poignant sense of composure as he peers over the precipice.

> Here on the world's edge at this hour I have
> Wondrously settled my life . . .
> The All is silent, only that fiddler fiddles.
> Dark one, already I stand in covenant with you . . .
> Let me feel, let there be revealed
> To this hale soul each wound . . .
> Do not stop, holy prayer, before then![47]

At the age of eighty-six, living "on the world's edge," exposed and helpless, Buber was pulling away from the "it" world and entering the breach of the "you." And I have a vague sense of what he is describing.

When I was lying prone in the hospital for weeks, with oxygen tubes in my nose, with wires coming out of my chest, arms, and legs, with beeping monitors and screens surrounding me, I too was on the world's edge. In this condition of being laid open and defenseless, it was not just fear that overwhelmed me, but love and compassion. I had a strong urge to call my two brothers immediately after my surgery to tell them how much I cared about them and how thankful I was to have them in my life. My girlfriend became my fiancée in the intensive care unit, after my blood clot. I felt as if I were seeing her for the first time with fresh eyes, as the beautiful, courageous, and tender being that she is. My parents, whom I spoke to every night in the hospital, revealed themselves in all of their generosity and devotion. The people in my life I ordinarily took for granted became luminous and fragile. And this extended beyond my family and friends, to include colleagues, neighbors, and even complete strangers at the supermarket or gas station. The masks of the "it" world came off and I sensed how defenseless and dependent we all are; and this made me love even more. But, as the weeks and months passed in my recovery, as my body healed and I returned to work, the trauma dimmed, and unfortunately so did my newfound capacity for compassion. As I continued to get stronger, I noticed the ego and its protective shell resurfacing. I was being slowly pulled back into the "it" world, absorbed once again in the shallow contentment of my career, my research, my fitness and physical appearance. Heidegger refers to this as "temptation" (*Versuchung*), a condition in which we are seduced by the comforts of everyday life, "sedated" (*beruhigt*) by its routines and the illusion of predictability and security they create.[48] But, as I was being tempted away, I began to miss the feeling of vulnerability, the sense of not holding back and of being wholly present with others that emerged spontaneously in the wake of my heart attack. This is when the existentialist is such a valuable teacher, reminding us that the ego is a fiction and that grasping for thing-like security is ultimately a sucker's game. In many ways, writing this book is my effort to resist temptation, to remind myself that I am inexorably helpless and alone, and that others confront the same lonely dread. It is the human predicament. To be true to ourselves, then, we have to face this predicament, affirm it, even love it. As Buber says, "[l]et us love the actual world that never wishes to be annulled, but love it in all its terror."[49] It is loving and not holding back that allow us to reach across the terrible abyss, touch the other, and say: "I am with you."

7

This Life Countless Times

How could I not be grateful for my whole life?

Friedrich Nietzsche

By any measure, Nietzsche suffered greatly throughout his life. He was riddled with physical ailments, digestive issues, myopia, shaky nerves, insomnia, and blinding headaches that forced him to resign from his professorship at the University of Basel at the age of thirty-five and left him dependent on an arsenal of medications such as morphine, chloral hydrate, and Veronal.[1] Lou Salomé, the only woman he ever loved, rejected his marriage proposal (twice). And the father he adored died at thirty-six of a "softening of the brain," as his condition was labeled, which abandoned Nietzsche to a controlling mother and a duplicitous, anti-Semitic sister. The combination yielded a "consummate machine of hell" for the young boy.[2] Nietzsche refers to his own life as a "*tragic* catastrophe," and this grim portrait would suggest that he spent his last days and weeks filled with bitterness and resentment, sick, isolated, and largely deserted by his friends.[3] But it was just the opposite.

Nietzsche was overflowing with gratitude, writing in his autobiography *Ecce Homo*: "I do not in the least want anything to be different from what it is; I myself do not want to become different."[4] At forty-four, just before suffering a total nervous breakdown that produced the crippling dementia from which he would never recover, he reflects on a life that would quickly come to an end.

> On this perfect day, when everything is ripening and not only the grape turns brown, the eye of the sun just fell upon my life: I looked back, I looked forward, and never saw so many good things at once. It was not for nothing that I buried my forty-fourth year today; I had the *right* to bury it . . . *How could I fail to be grateful to my whole life?*—and so I tell my life to myself.[5]

Here Nietzsche introduces a core piece of existentialist wisdom. If we are to be honest and true to ourselves, we must accept and affirm life *as it is*, without the illusory comforts of God, moral absolutes, or an afterlife. The aim is simply to say "Yes!" to this life, to embrace with gratitude everything that is, has been, and will be in our brief time on earth, including all of the loss, pain, and grief that comes with it.

There has been extensive empirical research on the health-promoting benefits of gratitude. Several studies suggest that gratitude can improve interpersonal relationships, emotional resilience, and sleep habits and can contribute to alleviating symptoms of depression and anxiety.[6] Indeed, as I was recovering from my heart attack, I came across research that suggests that the practice of taking time to focus on what we are thankful for actually enhances cardiovascular health, reduces inflammation, and improves heart rhythm by lowering stress.[7] More importantly, cross-sectional surveys indicate that the experience of gratitude is at its lowest in middle-aged and young adults but reaches its peak in old age.[8] And these findings don't necessarily correlate with positive life circumstances. Indeed, often those who have suffered the most are the ones who have the strongest gratitude skills and are more accepting of the experience of disability, illness, and death that comes in our final years.[9] The journalist John Leland witnessed this remarkable capacity in Fred, the resilient eighty-seven-year-old war veteran I introduced earlier.

> Fred was someone whose life had clearly taken a turn for the worse, an isolated old man with a bad heart and declining mobility. Yet Fred never saw himself that way. He was thankful for the gift of another day, for a visitor, for a hot meal, for a sunny afternoon he couldn't go out to enjoy. More than almost anyone I've met, Fred lived in the moment of gratitude for the pleasures he could still enjoy. The pains, he insisted, were temporary. He didn't worry about tomorrow, except to the extent of wanting to be around to enjoy it.[10]

For Fred, "life itself was reason to give thanks."[11] And this is Nietzsche's message: it suggests that gratitude is a virtue, that gratitude is the key to being true to oneself and to living a good life, because it opens us to who we are and makes it possible for us to accept our existence as a whole.

Here we see the mistake of asking to whom or for what we should be grateful.[12] The question is misplaced. It is not that we are grateful to particular people or for particular circumstances in our life—to our parents, to our friends, or for our good health. The point, for Nietzsche, is to broaden and expand ourselves, to be grateful and love *all of it*, not just life's gifts and the advantages one owes to other people, but the suffering as well. It is easy to be grateful for the kindness of strangers; but in Nietzsche's view we also have to be grateful for their cruelty. The point of gratitude is to go beyond the simple binary of good and evil, to recognize that life is tender *and* violent, creative *and* destructive, and to reflect deeply on how all these experiences shape us. So we must give thanks to the sadistic boss, the painful divorce, the cancer diagnosis, the agonizing missteps of our children, and the loss of loved ones. And we have to accept and acknowledge our own darker impulses, our petty insecurities, cruelties, and weaknesses; we have to affirm every aspect of our being, "*every* truth, even the simple, bitter, ugly, repulsive, unchristian, immoral truths ... For such truths do exist."[13] Rilke makes a similar point, writing: "Whoever does not at some point absolutely affirm and even rejoice fully in the dreadfulness of life will never lay claim to the inexpressible powers of our existence; he will pass through life along the periphery and will have been, once the decision has been cast, neither one of the living nor one of the dead."[14]

The aim here is to show that it's not enough to just endure this life. We must embrace it all and, according to Nietzsche, live as if each of the disastrous and blessed events that make us who we are will be returned to us over and over again, in the exact same way, for eternity. This would be "the heaviest weight" to carry, and in *The Gay Science* he describes it in a powerful thought experiment.

What if one day or one night a demon slinked after you into your loneliest loneliness and said to you: "This life, as you live it now and as you have lived it, you will have to live it once more and countless times more. And there will be nothing new about it, but every pain and every pleasure, and every thought and sigh, and everything unspeakably small and great in your life must come back to you, and all in the same series and sequence. ... The eternal hourglass of existence turned over and over again—and you with it, you, mote of dust." If that thought took control of you, it would change you as you are, and maybe shatter you.[15]

In Nietzsche's eyes, the thought of "eternal recurrence," of repeatedly living through all the boredom, catastrophe, and humiliation that life throws at us is too much for most of us to bear. Nietzsche himself shuddered at the thought of endlessly revisiting the unpleasant circumstances of his life, including his own family. "I confess," he writes, "that the most profound objection to 'eternal recurrence,' my truly *devastating* idea, is that of my mother and sister."[16] We are generally unable or unwilling to overcome ourselves and carry the full weight of our existence. But Nietzsche's "overman" (*Übermensch*) doesn't turn away from the demon's proposal. He responds: "You are a god and I have never heard anything more godlike."[17]

If recent empirical studies on gratitude are anything to go by, old age may bring with it some of the essential strengths of the overman, including an enhanced ability to be thankful in the face of life's difficulties, to let go of feelings of resentment and guilt, and to understand and fully accept the rich ambiguity that makes us who we are. Beth, a ninety-year-old woman living in a long-term care facility, explains exactly this:

> What is most surprising to me is that, in some respects, I feel more fulfilled, more true to myself than I've ever felt in my life. I understand myself and others in ways I would not have been able to when I was younger. . . . I am better able to speak my mind, to feel seen and heard, and to recognize what I can share and with whom I can share it. I am also able to reflect on my limitations and be less prone to guilt and shame. I know at times I do go to dark places. But I have learned not to stay there. I understand that adapting to loss can be a major source of strength and growth.[18]

Overflowing with gratitude, Beth appears to embody the spirit of what Nietzsche calls "the great health." She affirms the world as it is—"a world so over-rich in what is beautiful, strange, questionable, terrible, and divine."[19] And she admits that the one thing that matters above all is to "become who you are."[20] To be ungrateful about any of the choices or contingencies that shape us is, then, a sign of sickness, tantamount to a moral defect. But the skill of gratitude that emerges in old age also reveals a difficult truth: we are not masterful, self-reliant subjects but vulnerable and dependent beings, indebted to others for help. To be grateful is an exercise in humility, of coming to grips with our own dependence. And this is a theme explored extensively by someone who could be said to be Nietzsche's kindred spirit: the Russian novelist Fyodor Dostoevsky.[21]

In his famous novella *Notes from the Underground*, Dostoevsky introduces us to the "underground man," a reflexively stubborn and toxic anti-hero who tells his readers that the human being "is monstrously ungrateful!

Phenomenally ungrateful. In fact, I believe that the best definition of man is the ungrateful biped."[22] Against the traditional view that praises gratitude as a virtue essential to human flourishing and moral character, the underground man suggests that deep down we actually abhor the feeling of gratitude because it undermines the sense we have of our own autonomy and exposes our fundamental dependence on others.[23] For the underground man, the only thing that should matter and define us as human beings is freedom, "our own free unfettered choice," even if this choice is destructive and leads to our own alienation and misery. He reminds the reader that "what man wants is simply independent choice, whatever that independence may cost and wherever it may lead. And choice, of course, *the devil only knows what choice.*"[24] To be ungrateful is thus a way for the underground man to assert his free will, to express his individuality and power, and to convey to others that he doesn't need them. This equation pushes him into bizarre and self-destructive behavior. If he is sick, he refuses to see the doctor; if he is at a social gathering, he acts in outrageous and embarrassing ways; if someone reaches out to him in tenderness and love, he lashes out in cruelty.[25] These expressions of ingratitude spiral in a crescendo in the underground man's relationship with Liza, a compassionate prostitute who takes pity on him. In the intimacy of their exchanges he opens up to her about his own suffering and humiliations, but quickly realizes that the confession threatens his autonomy; it exposes his vulnerability and his longing to be loved and cared for. Instead of gratitude, the underground man feels humiliation and powerlessness and is overcome by a homicidal rage.[26]

A horrible spite against her suddenly surged up in my heart; I believe I could have killed her ... I had been humiliated, so I wanted to humiliate; I had been treated like a rag, so I wanted to show my power ... Power, power was what I wanted, sport was what I wanted, I wanted to wring out your tears, your humiliation, your hysteria—that was what I wanted.[27]

Dostoevsky presents the underground man as an ideological type, an extreme incarnation of the psychic tensions that emerged in mid-nineteenth-century Russia as the country was undergoing a period of rapid modernization. During that time, an older way of life, rooted in a sense of belongingness and close-knit religious communities, was quickly being replaced by secular values, newly imported from western Europe. Central among these was the modern liberal idea that we are, at bottom, not communal beings who are vulnerable and interdependent but sovereign individuals, self-reliant subjects who affirm our power by means our own independent choices. And this is what makes the story so unnerving. Formed by the same values, readers can see a bit of themselves in the underground man's repellent pride and self-absorption. Dostoevsky says as much in the prologue to the *Notes*, when he claims the underground man "not only may, but positively must, exist in our society, when we consider the circumstances in the midst of which our society is formed."[28] And these circumstances contribute to our own anxieties about growing old. If we are socialized into thinking that we are atomistic and masterful egos in no way dependent on others, then how do we adjust when this self-image breaks down in the evening of life? Dostoevsky goes to great lengths to expose this modern view of the self as a sham and to show us that it does not result in flourishing and self-realization but in loneliness and self-destruction. In his greatest novel, *The Brothers Karamazov*, he describes the same attitude as a "terrible individualism."

> The isolation that prevails everywhere, above all in our age—has not fully developed, it has not reached its limit yet. For everyone strives to keep his individuality, everyone wants to secure the greatest possible fullness of life for himself. But in the meantime, all his efforts result not in attaining fullness of life but self-destruction, for instead of self-realization he ends up arriving at complete solitude ... He has trained himself not to believe in the help of others, in men and in humanity, and only trembles for fear that he should lose his money and the privileges he has won for himself ... But this terrible individualism must inevitably come to an end, and all will suddenly understand how unnaturally they are separated from one another.[29]

Dostoevsky portrays the underground man as a pathetic figure, a man trapped in a ceaseless struggle for mastery and self-affirmation. As such, he embodies an impoverished conception of freedom: his capricious rebellion against anything that might limit or constrain him has produced his own bondage. "What do we see in this freedom?" writes Dostoevsky. "Nothing but slavery and self-destruction."[30] As an ideological type, the underground man "distorts" our own human nature.[31] For Dostoevsky, true freedom emerges when we release or free ourselves from our own pride and selfishness for the sake of something higher. This occurs through an act of "self-emptying," *kenosis*—a term used in theology to refer to Christ's act of submission to humiliation and suffering in order to obey God's will.[32] Dostoevsky envisions this kind of submission as one that emulates Christ as an archetype. It is rooted in a way of being that lets go of the ego in order to adopt an attitude of humility, self-sacrifice, and gratitude for the love and compassion of others. His aim is to show that we are not self-reliant subjects but fragile beings who are fundamentally bound together in defenselessness and vulnerability, so that "we are all responsible to all and for all."[33]

Dostoevsky's critique of liberal individualism becomes more important as we move into our later years and struggle to keep up with constructed expectations of autonomy and self-sufficiency. Because these expectations form the normative background of our lives, it becomes exceedingly difficult to reach out, to ask for and receive help from others. We remain, in the words of the underground man, "the ungrateful biped" because we reflexively see ourselves as encapsulated volitional egos, as beings who are—and must be—in control. If this picture is true, how are we supposed to "shake off the habits"[34] and learn the skill of *kenosis*, cope with our own disability and decline in old age, or embody the humility necessary for accepting aid and compassion from a family member or a healthcare worker?[35] A theme that recurs in Dostoevsky's novels is the idea that giving *and* accepting charity are acts essential to any *imitatio Christi*, that is, to any attempt to live in the imitation of Christ.[36] In *Crime and Punishment*, for example, the murderous Raskolnikov embodies many of the same ideological traits as the underground man. In his world, what matters above all is "freedom and power, and most importantly power! Over all trembling creatures, over the whole ant heap! . . . That's the goal! Remember it!"[37] But, unlike the underground man, Raskolnikov is not an anti-hero; he is redeemed in the end by the realization that his toxic individualism and his desire for self-affirmation are (and have always been) the source of his loneliness and despair.[38] With the religious wisdom of Sonia to guide him, he comes to understand his inherent vulnerability and weakness and, in order to live in the image of Christ, he recognizes the need to humble himself and graciously accept the charity of others.

As the embodiment of our shared vulnerability, Dostoevsky turns on its head the lofty image of Christ as an authoritative and exalted God-man. Speaking through the character of Father Zosima in *The Brothers Karamazov*, he draws on a popular folk legend in Russia, portraying Christ as a meek and powerless figure, a poor beggar who wanders the countryside looking for charity. The message is that it is through acts of selfless love and kindness, both by giving and by receiving, that we are able to let go of the ego and our longing for power and self-affirmation and to begin to interact with Christ himself.[39] In the aftermath of my heart attack, I struggled deeply with this idea. My self-image has been shaped profoundly by the modern assumptions of liberal individualism, and I have long regarded myself as a willful, self-reliant subject. And even though this image came crashing down in the hospital, my initial experience in the emergency room wasn't formed by a sense of gratitude for the life-saving care I received, but by a sense of embarrassment, shame, and humiliation at the loss of my own independence and strength. Yet it was in these moments of helplessness that I came to understand what Dostoevsky meant by grace.

There was a particularly dark day in the intensive care unit when my cardiologist diagnosed me with a dangerous heart rhythm called ventricular tachycardia, which made me susceptible to sudden cardiac death and suggested that I may need to have an electronic defibrillator implanted in my chest to resuscitate me. I was devastated by this news. Later that evening, a middle-aged nursing assistant came into my room. She must have sensed my despair and, perhaps to put me at ease, she began asking a few simple questions about my life, where was I from, was I married, what did I do for work. She then started to tell me a bit about herself, how she ended up in Florida, her job at the hospital, her eldest son's love of basketball. But then she went deeper, gently opening up about her own personal struggles, her depression, her congenital heart trouble, and about wanting to commit suicide earlier in her life. In the midst of this uncanny expression of vulnerability, I felt safe and understood and began to confess to her my own feelings of anxiety and helplessness. She listened to me, and when I finished, she gave me a knowing smile, and wordlessly pulled down the collar of her shirt and pointed at the clavicle scar from her own implanted defibrillator. Before leaving, she sang a quiet rendition of an African American spiritual to lift me up. I never saw her again, but it felt like a moment of grace. I was left sobbing that night, overcome by her compassion, by her capacity to suffer *with me*.

In his work, Dostoevsky makes it clear that selflessly caring for others is a virtuous act, but we see now that his point goes deeper: acknowledging our own powerlessness and dependency in the face of suffering is not a sign of weakness or of something to be ashamed of, but one of spiritual strength. It is the lack of gratitude that makes the underground man such a pitiful figure. Walled in by his own pride, he is closed off from the redemptive power of human tenderness and connection. As if issuing a warning to the reader, he confesses: "I was incapable of love . . . With me loving meant tyrannizing and showing my moral superiority. I have never been able to imagine any other sort of love," and that is how "I have succeeded in destroying myself."[40] According to Dostoevsky, we are acting with grace and courage when, in times of sickness and in old age, we place our lives in the hands of others. To give oneself over in this way is itself an expression of Christ-like divinity, an act that "subdues" our "proud and wanton will" and allows us to see fully that we are not self-sufficient egos but relational beings, who are ultimately defenseless and condemned to suffer without the freely given love and compassion of others.[41]

8

Held Out into Nothing

Where is it? What death?

Leo Tolstoy

Of all the meditations on death in existentialist literature, it is without question Tolstoy's *The Death of Ivan Ilych* that reigns supreme. It is the story of a superficial bourgeois magistrate whose entire life has been pulled along by the shallows of social convention. He is alienated from his children, his marriage is void of intimacy, and his primary ambitions are centered around making money, throwing cocktail parties, playing cards with his friends, and furnishing his new house in such a way as to appear wealthier than he is. But, as he's hanging expensive curtains in the living room one day, he slips and injures himself. He bruises from the accident, and the bruise gets worse and worse. He soon realizes that something is gravely wrong. Gripped by anxiety, he seeks help from leading medical specialists. But the physicians don't see Ivan Ilych as a frightened and vulnerable human being. From the dispassionate standpoint of medical science, they see him as an object, an interesting set of symptoms to be managed and controlled. For Ivan, the detached and calculated treatment he receives in the various clinics is not only cold and dehumanizing. It is dishonest. The physicians know he is dying, but they are unwilling or unable to talk honestly and openly about it. Tolstoy writes:

> What tormented Ivan Ilych most was the deception, the lie, which for some reason they all accepted, that he was not dying but was simply ill, and that he only needed to keep quiet and undergo a treatment and then something very good would result . . . The deception tortured him—their not wishing to admit what they all knew and what he knew, but wanting to lie to him concerning his terrible condition, and wishing and forcing him to participate in that lie.[1]

In his book *Being Mortal: Medicine and What Matters in the End*, the endocrine surgeon Atul Gawande argues that modern medicine hasn't evolved much since Ivan Ilych's day. Indeed, the lies seem to be getting worse. Physicians today are trained in medical schools to see the person in reductive terms of mechanistic functioning, and they focus on biological disease processes and sophisticated procedures to manage and control dysfunction. But Ivan's story reminds us that aging and dying are not technical problems; they are inescapable givens of the human condition, and physicians perpetuate the lie by treating them as medical issues. As Gawande writes,

> Modern scientific capability has profoundly altered the course of human life. People live longer and better than at any other time in history. But scientific advances have turned the processes of aging and dying into medical

experiences, matters to be managed by health care professionals. And we in the medical world have proved alarmingly unprepared for it.[2]

The myth of control in medicine is so pervasive and entrenched today that it is actually illegal to record old age as the cause of death.[3] Old age can't be a diagnosis because there must be a medical cause—stroke, heart attack, or respiratory failure—and, if medical science can control these causes, then perhaps one day it can control death as well.[4]

As our bodily systems weaken and break down in old age, we are drawn increasingly into the medical industrial complex and its vast system of management and maintenance, succumbing to what Gawande calls the myriad "patch jobs" employed to extend life. The Promethean ethos is embodied in the way the physician works to "reduce the blood pressure here, beat back the osteoporosis there, control this disease, track that one, replace a failed joint, valve, piston, watch the central processing unit gradually give out."[5] For the existentialist, the goal here is not merely to preserve and prolong biological life artificially, but to deny the reality of death. As the German philosopher Hans-Georg Gadamer writes, "[t]his process culminates in the gradual disappearance of death. The anesthetic drugs developed by modern pharmaceutics can completely sedate the suffering person. The artificial maintenance of vegetative functions of the organism makes the person into a link in the chain of causal processes."[6] The result is that older persons are often excluded from attending to and participating in the experience of their own death. And this, more than anything, was what Ivan

Ilych longed for as his condition worsened and he came to the horrifying realization that the end was near. He wanted the physicians to be honest with him, to treat him as a person not as an object, not just to blunt his pain with morphine but to help him understand, accept, and give meaning to his life and death.

Interestingly, it was not the high-priced medical specialists that helped Ivan Ilych move in the direction of acceptance and integration. It was his manservant, a young peasant named Gerasim, who treated him with tenderness and compassion. Grounded in the simplicity and tight-knit community of Russian peasant life, Gerasim was uncorrupted by his master's bourgeois values and was honest and clear-sighted about Ilych's fate because he knew it would also be his fate one day.

> Gerasim alone did not lie; everything showed that he alone understood the facts of the case and did not consider it necessary to disguise them, but simply felt sorry for his emaciated and enfeebled master ... He did not think his work burdensome, because he was doing it for a dying man and hoped someone would do the same for him when his time came.[7]

Ilych was humiliated and debased by his condition; he was weak and frail, unable to pull up his own trousers after using the commode. But Gerasim was unfazed. He picked him up, held his legs, and rubbed his feet for hours to relieve the pain. "We shall all of us die," he told his master with a warm smile, "so why should I grudge a little trouble."[8]

Gerasim heals the dying man in a way that modern medicine can't. He reveals that the denial of death isolates us from each other, while honesty and acceptance create bonds of connection rooted in our shared vulner-ability. And this leads to a transformation for Ilych, as he sheds the surface vanities of his former self and begins to see what is truly significant in life. *The Death of Ivan Ilych* reminds us of why it is far more important to come to terms with death at the end of life than to try to control it through medical technology. As Gadamer asks, "[t]o what extent may the doctor seek to ease the patient's suffering when what is thereby taken away is not only the patient's pain but also their 'person,' their freedom and responsibility for their own life, and ultimately even awareness of their own death?"[9]

The American Medical Association (AMA) today relies on a very narrow and reductive interpretation of death, according to which you are dead if you have sustained "either irreversible cessation of circulatory and respiratory function" or "irreversible cessation of all functions of the entire brain, including the brain stem."[10] But for the existentialist, as we have seen, death has little to do with the end of respiratory function or brain activity. It occurs when we are no longer open and receptive to the solicitations of the world, when we can no longer relate to others, take a stand on our life and give it meaning. We can be dead, on this view, even as the heart continues to pump, as neurotransmitters fire, as lungs contract and expand. There is, as Nietzsche says, a fate far worse than biological death, and that is to be dead while we are alive, to "vegetate on in cowardly dependence on physicians and medicaments after the meaning of life . . . has been lost."[11] This is Gawande's point, and he suggests that, with the emer-gence of hospice and palliative care in recent decades, physicians are finally beginning to accept the limits of what they can control and to incorporate the wisdom of existentialism: that "patients have priorities beyond merely being safe and living longer, that the chance to shape one's story is essential to sustaining meaning in life."[12] Cardiologists today recognize that "patients have the right to have their doctors turn off their pacemakers if they want."[13] The result is that physicians see their responsibilities extending beyond the physiological health and survival of their elderly patients. Such responsibilities also involve helping those on the brink to understand and make sense of their situation, to confront their fears, and to ask themselves how they would like to live their remaining days and weeks.[14] This kind of help allows the person, even in a terminal state, to continue to exist with a measure of autonomy and agency. But, more importantly, it opens us up to the truth of our condition in old age, that we have run up against our temporal limits, that we are no longer, in Sartre's words, "the being who hurls himself toward the future" because the future is gone.[15] And the task now is to detach oneself or let go, to prepare for death, to try to become, for lack of a better word, "nothing."

In youth and middle age we spend most of our time trying to make ourselves into "something." We get married, start a family, build a career, accumulate wealth, all the while pulled along by the idea that this will create an existence that is enduring and real. This is the life that Ivan Ilych was trapped in. Distracted and lost in surface materialism and in careerist ambitions, he was, like most of us, oblivious to what really matters in life. It is for this reason that Tolstoy describes Ilych's life as "most simple and most ordinary and therefore *most terrible*."[16] It is his illness that shakes him out of self-deception; his pleasant and well-ordered world collapses and he realizes: "Maybe I did not live as I should have."[17] Awake for the first time in his life, Ilych begins to shed the masks of successful magistrate, charming party host, bourgeois homeowner. He realizes that it was the masks that were oppressing him all along, and they were now "all dropping away at once from two sides, from ten sides, and from all sides."[18] In the process of self-emptying, he is released, left naked and exposed. Merging with the void, he is becoming nothing, and, in the process, the fear of death, and even death itself, disappear.

> "And death . . . where is it?"
> He sought his former accustomed fear of death and did not find it. "Where is it? What death?" There was no fear because there was no death.
> In place of death there was light.
> "So that's what it is!" he suddenly exclaimed aloud. "What joy!"[19]

Terminal illness accelerated Ivan Ilych's awakening. Old age brings it to us more gradually, in stages. The Hindu tradition is instructive here, in that it identifies four distinct stages of life (*ashramas*).[20] The first stage, *brahmacharya*, is the time of youth and young adulthood. This is a stage of learning, of being a student, when one is educated in a trade or a discipline. The second stage, *grihastha*, is the time of building a household, establishing a career, having children, and purchasing a home. For the existentialist, it is here that we often fall into a prolonged state of self-deception, as happened to Ilych: we become attached to our occupations, our possessions, our physical appearance, our sexual appetites.

We cling to this stage as long as possible because it covers over the nothingness at the core of our existence and creates the illusion that we are solid and secure.[21] But, as we get older and the children leave the house, the marriage implodes, or the body begins to break down, we may experience a crisis, since we sense that our future is contracting and our time is limited. This opens us to the possibility of awakening, to *vanaprastha*: the stage of retirement, of abandoning the sensual, materialistic, and ego-driven desires that consumed us in *grihastha*. It is the beginning of a more spiritual path, a movement toward liberation (*moksha*), toward being freed from the cycle of worldly appetites and ambitions; we come to realize that our craving for things like professional success was an illusion all along, that prestige was quite literally "a magic trick," a prestidigitation. This is the enlightened stage of old age, an Indian summer that can last for decades; but it was one that Ilych missed out on. He was unprepared and horrified as his illness in midlife pulled him straight from the earthly enticements of *grihastha* to *sannyasa*, the stage of renunciation.

If *vanaprastha* is a preparatory stage in the *ashrama* system, then *sannyasa* is the final stage of life, the stage of the so-called oldest old. When there are no more medical interventions or patch jobs to perform, when there is no desire, no possession or identity to hold on to, one is finally ready for *sannyasa*, ready to detach oneself from the world. In the Hindu tradition, detachment involves a kind of radical asceticism. One renounces attachments altogether, including to one's home and property, and focuses entirely on the bliss of *moksha*.[22] For the existentialist, this stage involves a readiness to die, to be willing to lose one's being and merge with nothingness. This is where we finally turn away from Dylan Thomas' defiant charge to "rage against the dying of the light." There is no longer any need to rage against death or to cling to life. For the oldest old, the aim is to be released, to be absorbed by the darkness, to welcome it. It is, as the French philosopher Jacques Maritain writes,

> to enter a world where there is no longer anything to protect us, and finally, it is to take leave, in a way, of the human race—to not want to be a man. There is the great night, the night which stirs, and the desire to lose one's being.[23]

In this final stage, losing one's being is not something to be afraid of. As Rilke suggests, death is merely the other side of life, a side that remains largely hidden when we are lost in the worldly shallows of youth and middle age. It indicates that "we are *full*," that the glorious and tragic mission of existence has been completed.[24] This is why Rilke says that "we must learn to die," and we see now how growing old can be viewed as a kind of progressive instruction, of "learn[ing] to die slowly."[25] In his *Book of Hours*, Rilke captures this sense of being ready for death, even welcoming it.

> I'm slipping. I'm slipping away
> like sand
> slipping through fingers . . .
> I want to die. Leave me alone.
> I feel I am almost there—
> Where the great terror can dismember me.[26]

What is missing in this account is one of the ur-principles of existentialism, namely that the confrontation with one's own death is invariably accompanied by a visceral sense of anxiety or dread. But, for the oldest old, it is not the screaming horror of Ivan Ilych that manifests itself, but rather a sense of serenity and calm. We see now that death is not a reference to a medical or biological event. It is an experience that we live through, that erupts when we are no longer able to meaningfully engage with the world, when we lose our grip on the purposive roles and projects that sustain our identities. On this view, Ilych is dying not so much because his physical body is breaking down but because the secure world he's been clinging to has suddenly collapsed and he is left alone to face the void—what Heidegger calls "the bare 'that-it-is' in the 'nothing' of the world."[27] Ilych did not have the slow instruction of growing old to prepare him, to help him loosen his grip and see through the illusion that his existence was something real and thing-like. In the final stage of life, we are well on our way to being released from the world, exposed to the nothing, to Heidegger's "open region" (*das Offene*), the dizzying and vast space of mystery and silence that delimits and undergirds our existence. At this stage we are no longer fleeing the nothing with our busy projects, willfully trying to be something. Indeed, there is an absence of willing altogether; willing is replaced by a sense of detachment and letting be. Held out into the nothing, anxiety is transformed into "a peculiar calm" (*eigentümliche Ruhe*) that Heidegger associates with a primordial freedom.[28]

> Freedom now reveals itself as letting beings be ... To let be—that is, to let beings be as the beings that they are—means to engage oneself with the open region and its openness into which every being comes to stand, bringing that openness as it were, along with itself.[29]

But Heidegger makes it clear that freedom, as letting be, does not mean that we are disengaged, indifferent, or neglectful of beings, and it's not to be confused with passivity or quietism either. Rather, "[t]o let be is to engage oneself with beings," but it is an engagement that is no longer grounded in anxious delusions of the willful subject who has mastery and control over things.[30] It is a way of being that understands and accepts that existence is fundamentally contingent, unsettled, and "groundless" (*grundlos*), that the nothing is "always latent in being-in-the-world," always lurking behind and beneath us.[31] When we enter the winter phase of the oldest old, "we release ourselves into the nothing, which is to say we liberate ourselves from those idols everyone has and to which they are wont to go cringing."[32] For Heidegger, being liberated in this way illuminates an extraordinary philosophical truth: that in the brief flash of our existence we are given an opportunity to dwell on this fragile earth and witness the fact that "there is something rather than nothing, there are beings and *we ourselves are in their midst.*"[33]

Recent gerontological studies in advanced old age lend support to this Heideggerian interpretation. In one investigation in particular, researchers interviewed residents of the city of Jyväskylä in central Finland who were eighty years old and collected narrative reports of their experience.[34] A ten-year follow-up study was conducted for those who were still alive at the age of ninety. Researchers observed a marked transformation during this ten-year period. What became clear was that the ninety-year-old participants had crossed an existential boundary; they were far more liberated from their attachments to the world and more open and receptive to the nothing. Researchers observed a notable sense of calm and an absence of death anxiety.

> They seemed different from what they were before. They seemed confident and at ease with themselves: there was no sense of concern about themselves, about their significant others, about the world around them. They just seemed to be adjusting to the changes that were happening in themselves.[35]

This sense of releasement extended to their relationship with time. They were more present than they had been a decade earlier, no longer projecting forward into the future, in an attempt to hold on to something. "It seems that [they] had stopped time. Their perspective on the future had changed. They seemed unconcerned both by their own age and by the finitude of their own life ... They had stopped trying to rush things or to stop or catch up with time."[36] Participants were even dissociating themselves from their own bodies. In their eighties, complaints about bodily pain, discomfort, and illness had been a central part of their story. But in their nineties, even though their bodies were far more compromised and burdensome, "they no longer seem troubled" "and they hardly mentioned their illnesses or pains."[37] The overarching message of the study was that these elders had a heightened sense of the impermanence and poignancy of life and were largely unconcerned with things they no longer needed. They understood who they were and exhibited a radical tolerance and acceptance of the underlying mystery and unsettledness of existence. In Heidegger's words, they were "letting themselves be transformed."[38]

In his reflections on what he knew to be the last days of his long life, Oliver Sacks captures the Heideggerian insights of this Finnish study. Sacks was well into his eighties and was dying from cancer. The future had closed down for him and he was withdrawing from the affairs of the world. "I shall no longer look at the *NewsHour* every night. I shall no longer pay any attention to politics or arguments about global warming."[39] But he makes it clear that this withdrawal "is not indifference but detachment," a kind of engaged freedom that releases him from the "factious urgencies of earlier days," deepening his awareness of the exquisite transiency of things, and allowing him to feel intensely present and alive.[40] Although there is still fear of the unknown, the overwhelming sentiment for Sacks is one of thankfulness, of appreciation for being given the opportunity to complete the extraordinary journey of life. Heidegger himself went back to Old English and found an interesting convergence between the words "to think" (*thencan*) and "to thank" (*thancian*).[41] To let go of things was, for him, a kind of "meditative thinking" (*besinnliche Denken*) that gives thanks; it was "releasement toward things and openness to mystery."[42] Instead of fleeing or denying the nothing, we calmly turn toward it, give thanks, and "let ourselves become involved with beautiful, mysterious, and gracious things."[43] At the end of his life, Sacks too was thinking and giving thanks in this way.

> My predominant feeling is one of gratitude. I have loved and been loved; I have been given much and I have given something in return; I have read and traveled and thought and written. I have had intercourse with the world ... Above all, I have been a sentient being, a

thinking animal, on this beautiful planet, and that in itself has been an enormous privilege and adventure.[44]

In my last day of cardiac rehab, six weeks after my heart attack, I was in a very dark place. I was taking multiple blood thinners and arrhythmia and blood pressure medications; I was wearing an external defibrillator around my chest; and I was suffering from paralyzing agoraphobia. My life had imploded. The projects that held my identity together were in chaos and I was numb to the world, dying because I was unable *to be*. As I shuffled out of the rehab center on the sprawling Health Park campus in Fort Myers, I saw an unsettling image. By a small lake near the residential complex was an old man in a wheelchair, all alone in the hot Florida sun, with his head tilted way back toward the sky. I was horrified. The old man looked dead. Although I quickly saw that a nursing assistant was sitting on a bench nearby engrossed in her phone, I was still concerned. I decided to cross the street and walk toward the lake to check on him. As I got closer, I noticed he wasn't asleep or unconscious, he was watching a massive flock of black birds swooping in and out of the trees above him. And as I got closer still, I saw that his eyes were wide and clear and he had a rapturous smile on his face. Suddenly feeling silly standing next to him, I asked him what he was doing. He turned to me beaming, and all he said was, "I'm looking." For some reason, these simple words shook me. They still do. I was flooded with emotion and tears welled up in my eyes as I turned away and walked back toward my car.

Two years later I was in New York City with my wife, for a conference. Although I was still taking numerous medications and had a heightened sense of body vigilance, the trauma of the heart attack had begun to fade and I was back to my regular cycling and gym routine. I had tried to make it in New York in an earlier life, but it pitilessly chewed me up and spat me out. From that point on, whenever I returned for a visit, I would get anxious, haunted by my past failure and overwhelmed by the city's disjointed density and the unnerving stimulation of its sights and sounds. But this trip was different. My heart attack and the confrontation with death had somehow changed me. The old ruminating fears had softened, replaced by an enhanced sense of being open and present. I enjoyed the food, the architecture, and the crazed street scenes in a way I never had before. It was all New York, gloriously chaotic and unpredictable. Sitting in Washington Square Park in the evening one night, we listened to a musician who had somehow dragged a grand piano into the park and surrounded it with candles. He proceeded to play a tender rendition of Beethoven's "Moonlight Sonata" under the stars. I was filled with gratitude and overcome with an exhilarating sense of freedom. My thoughts drifted back to the incident with the old man in the wheelchair. I smiled and thought to myself, "I'm looking."

Appendix
The Existentialists

Hannah Arendt (1906–1975). Born in Linden, Germany, Arendt studied with Martin Heidegger and Karl Jaspers, respectively at the universities of Marburg and Heidelberg, before fleeing the Nazis and ultimately emigrating to the United States. Her work addresses existence in the public sphere, explores the nature of evil in totalitarian regimes, and examines the essential importance of political action or praxis. Some of her most notable works are the essay "What Is Existenz Philosophy?" (1946), *The Origins of Totalitarianism* (1951), *The Human Condition* (1958), and *Eichmann in Jerusalem* (1964).

Simone de Beauvoir (1908–1986). Born in Paris and educated at the Sorbonne and the École Normale Supérieure, Beauvoir was a powerful voice in the rise of French existentialism and pioneered a feminist approach to the human condition through her hugely influential 1949 work *The Second Sex*, which explores how a woman's freedom and capacity for self-creation are limited and constrained by patriarchal forces and how she is often complicit in her own objectification. Beauvoir was awarded the Prix Goncourt for her 1954 novel *The Mandarins* and is the only major figure in existentialism to critically engage with the experience of old age, which she did in her monumental work *The Coming of Age* (1970).

Martin Buber (1878–1965). Born in Vienna, Buber studied philosophy and art at the universities of Vienna, Berlin, Leipzig, and Zürich and spent the latter part of his career teaching at the Hebrew University of Jerusalem. A member of the Zionist movement, he drew on the resources of Hasidic Judaism and other mystical traditions to critique forms of alienation in modern society and to develop a dialogical conception of human existence, most notably in his 1923 masterwork *I and Thou*.

Albert Camus (1913–1960). Born in what is now Dréan in French Algeria and educated at the University of Algiers, Camus was a prominent member of the Communist Party in France and Algeria. Deeply influenced by Nietzsche, he explored the inherent absurdity of existence, the philosophical problem of suicide, and the need to rebel against forms of social and political oppression. His most influential works are *The Stranger* (1942), *The Myth of Sisyphus* (1942), *The Plague* (1947), and *The Rebel* (1951). Camus was awarded the Nobel Prize in Literature in 1957.

Fyodor Dostoevsky (1821–1881). Born in Moscow, Dostoevsky studied engineering before pursuing a career as a writer and literary and political activist (for which he was arrested, sent to a Siberian prison camp, and subjected to a mock execution). His deeply psychological writings address problems of free will and human evil, the suffering inherent in secular individualistic societies, and the possibilities for spiritual redemption. His most influential novels and short stories include *The House of the Dead* (1862), *Notes from the Underground* (1864), *Crime and Punishment* (1866), and *The Brothers Karamazov* (1880).

Hans-Georg Gadamer (1900–2002). Born in Marburg, Germany and educated at the universities of Breslau, Freiburg, and Marburg, Gadamer was a student of Heidegger's and taught philosophy at Goethe University and the University of Heidelberg. He is known for pioneering an interpretative (or hermeneutic) account of human existence, according to which one exists not as a substance but as a dialogical process in the historically situated meanings that one projects for oneself. Influential works include *Truth and Method* (1960) and *The Idea of the Good in Platonic–Aristotelian Philosophy* (1978). His 1993 collection *The Enigma of Health* has had an enormous impact on existential approaches to health and illness.

Søren Kierkegaard (1813–1855). Born and raised in Copenhagen and educated in theology at the University of Copenhagen, Kierkegaard is widely considered to be the father of modern existentialism, as he engaged with core issues of religious faith, anxiety, guilt, and death. He often published under pseudonyms and employed a form of indirect communication to express the indeterminate and paradoxical aspects of the human condition.

His most influential works are *Either/Or* (1843), *Fear and Trembling* (1843), *The Concept of Anxiety* (1844), and *The Sickness unto Death* (1849).

Martin Heidegger (1889–1976). Born in Meßkirch, Germany and educated at the University of Freiburg, Heidegger taught at the universities of Marburg and Freiburg. His 1927 masterwork *Being and Time* is arguably the most significant contribution to existentialist philosophy, offering the first systematic analyses of everyday human existence, authenticity, and being toward death. Shaped by the work of nineteenth-century pioneers such as Kierkegaard and Nietzsche, his thought had an enormous impact on French existentialism. His most notable students included Hannah Arendt, Hans-George Gadamer, and Herbert Marcuse. He is widely considered to be the most influential and (because of his associations with Nazism) controversial philosopher of the twentieth century.

Gabriel Marcel (1889–1973). Born in Paris and educated at the Sorbonne, Marcel was a Christian existentialist; and he is the one who coined the term "existentialism" in 1943. His philosophy critiqued the instrumental and dehumanizing aspects of modern technocratic society and reflected on the importance of genuine communion between human beings, the salvific role of hope, and the acceptance of the fundamental mystery of existence. Notable works include *Being and Having* (1949), *The Mystery of Being* (1951), and *Homo Viator* (1962).

Jacques Maritain (1882–1973). Born in Paris and educated at the Sorbonne and the Collège de France,

Maritain was a Thomist philosopher who offered critiques of modernity and scientism and argued that being is grasped directly and immediately through intuition, in the act of existing. He forwarded an influential account of the human being as fundamentally self-creating. His social philosophy had an enormous impact on the Catholic Church and on the thought of Pope John Paul II in particular. Some of his more influential works include *The Degrees of Knowledge* (1932), *The Person and the Common Good* (1947), and, with his wife Raïssa Maritain, *The Situation of Poetry* (1955).

Maurice Merleau-Ponty (1908–1961). Born in Rochefort-sur-Mer, France and educated at the Sorbonne and the École Normale Supérieure, Merleau-Ponty taught philosophy at the Sorbonne and the Collège of France and, along with Beauvoir and Sartre, helped launch the influential journal of cultural criticism: *Les Temps Modernes*. He is most well known for groundbreaking interpretations of embodiment and perception, especially in his seminal 1945 work *Phenomenology of Perception*. His writings have had a significant impact on advances in developmental psychology, feminist phenomenology, and eco-phenomenology.

Friedrich Nietzsche (1844–1900). Born in Röcken, Germany, Nietzsche studied philology and theology at the University of Bonn and became a professor of classical philology at the University of Basel at the remarkable age of twenty-four, having completed neither a doctorate nor a habilitation. He left academe in his early thirties owing to poor health and proceeded to write some of his greatest works: *The Gay Science*

(1882), *Thus Spoke Zarathustra* (1883), and *Beyond Good and Evil* (1886). His thought engaged classic existential themes of nihilism, the loss of moral absolutes, the transgressive power of art, and the importance of self-overcoming.

José Ortega y Gasset (1883–1955). Born and educated in Madrid, Ortega y Gasset took his doctorate in philosophy from the University of Madrid, then continued his philosophical studies at a number of German universities. He is largely responsible for introducing existentialism to Latin America, in particular Argentina. His work examines the experience of alienation in mass society and develops an idea of existence as a dialectical tension or struggle for self-creation. His most notable works include *The Dehumanization of Art* (1925), *The Revolt of the Masses* (1930), and *History as a System* (1935).

Blaise Pascal (1623–1662). Born in Clermont-Ferrand, France, Pascal was a prodigious mathematician, physicist, and philosopher and is considered by many to be a proto-existentialist on account of his influential meditations on death, isolation, and the irrational logic (*logique de coeur*, "heart logic") of religious faith. His most notable contributions to existentialism are found in his posthumously published *Pensées* (1670).

Rainer Maria Rilke (1875–1926). Born in Prague, Rilke was an influential German language poet and writer whose semi-autobiographical 1910 novel *The Notebooks of Malte Laurids Brigge* became famous for engaging existentialist themes of freedom, death, and alienation. His extensive poems and letters, including *The Book of Hours* (1905), *Duino Elegies* (1922), *Sonnets to Orpheus* (1922), and *Letters to a Young Poet* (1929), had a major impact on a number of influential twentieth-century poets and writers.

Jean-Paul Sartre (1905–1980). Born in Paris and educated at the Sorbonne and the École Normale Supérieure, Sartre became a prominent public intellectual and the most famous spokesperson for French existentialism, developing influential conceptions of human freedom and responsibility and the structural antagonism of interpersonal relationships. His magnum opus *Being and Nothingness* (1943) is widely considered to be a canonical text, and the novella *Nausea* (1938), the play *No Exit* (1944), and the extended essay *Existentialism Is a Humanism* (1945, a lecture turned into a book) are existentialist classics. He won the Nobel Prize in Literature in 1964 but, famously, refused the prize because he did not want to be objectified as an "institution."

Paul Tillich (1886–1965). Born in Starzeddel, Germany and educated at the universities of Berlin, Tübingen, Breslau, and Halle-Wittenberg, Tillich served as professor of theology at a number of German universities before moving to the United States to teach. Influenced by Heidegger, he examined the question of what it means to be human and the courage involved in asking the question. As an ordained Lutheran minister, he also explored the importance of religious faith and developed an existentialist conception of God as the abysmal ground of being. His key works are *The Shaking of*

Foundations (1948), *The Courage to Be* (1952), and *The Dynamics of Faith* (1957).

Leo Tolstoy (1828–1910). Born on his family estate at Yasnaya Polyana outside of Tula, Russia, Tolstoy had a prominent lineage and studied law and oriental languages at Kazan University before leaving to pursue his writing career. His novels and short stories offer existential critiques of bourgeois conformism, illuminate the simple dignity of Russian peasant life, and address ultimate questions of human suffering and the meaning of life and death. His most influential works are *War and Peace* (1869), *Anna Karenina* (1878), and *The Death of Ivan Ilych* (1886).

Miguel de Unamuno (1864–1936). Born in Bilbao, Spain and educated at the Complutense University of Madrid, Unamuno was a hugely influential philosopher, poet, and novelist who served two terms as rector of the University of Salamanca. Deeply influenced by Kierkegaard, he challenged the authority of objective science and the idea that existence could be understood rationally. His most notable philosophical works are *The Tragic Sense of Life* (1912) and *The Agony of Christianity* (1931).

Irvin Yalom (b. 1931). Born in Washington DC and educated at George Washington University and at the Boston University School of Medicine, Yalom is a key figure in the development of existential approaches to psychology and psychotherapy. His clinical and theoretical work explores what he calls the "givens" of the human condition—death, freedom, isolation, and meaninglessness—and the role these givens play in the manifestation of psychopathology. His work *Existential Psychotherapy* (1980) is considered a classic in the field.

Notes

Notes to Introduction

1 John Leland, *Happiness Is a Choice you Make: Lessons from a Year among the Oldest Old* (New York: Sarah Crichton books, 2018), p. 29.

2 Friedrich Nietzsche, *The Gay Science*, translated by R. Polt. In C. Guignon and D. Pereboom (eds.), *Existentialism: Basic Writings* (Indianapolis, IN: Hackett, 2001), aphorisms 276 and 382.

3 Albert Camus, *The Rebel*, translated by A. Bower (New York: Vintage Books, 1956), p. 72.

4 Rainer Maria Rilke, *Letters to a Young Poet*, translated by R. Snell (Mineola, NY: Dover Publications, 1962), p. 12.

5 Søren Kierkegaard, *The Sickness unto Death*, translated by A. Hannay (New York: Penguin Books, 1989), p. 43.

6 Friedrich Nietzsche, *The Will to Power*, translated by W. Kaufmann (New York: Vintage Books, 1968), aphorism 370.

7 Simone de Beauvoir, *The Coming of Age*, translated by P. O'Brian (New York: W. W. Norton, 1996), p. 440.

8 James Hillman, *The Force of Character and the Lasting Life* (New York: Ballantine Books, 1999), p. 41.

9 Rainer Maria Rilke, *The Poet's Guide to Life*, translated by U. Baer (New York: Modern Library, 2005), p. 121.
10 Ibid., p. 117.

Notes to Chapter 1

1 Irvin Yalom, *Existential Psychotherapy* (New York: Basic Books, 1980), p. 98.
2 Lawrence Samuel, *Aging in America: A Cultural History*. (Philadelphia: University of Pennsylvania Press, 2017), p. 1.
3 Quoted in Lizzy Buchan, "Coronavirus: Downing Street Denies Claim Dominic Cummings Wanted to Protect the Economy over Elderly." *Independent*, March 22, 2020. https://www.independent.co.uk/news/uk/politics/dominic -cummings-boris-johnson-coronavirus-elderly-economy -a9417246.html.
4 Felicia Sonmez, "Texas Lt. Gov. Dan Patrick comes under fire for saying seniors should 'take a chance' on their own lives for the sake of grandchildren during coronavirus crisis." *Washington Post*, March 24, 2020. https://www .washingtonpost.com/politics/texas-lt-gov-dan-patrick- comes-under-fire-for-saying-seniors-should-take-a-chan ce-on-their-own-lives-for-sake-of-grandchildren-during -coronavirus-crisis/2020/03/24/e6f64858-6de6-11ea-b1 48-e4ce3fbd85b5_story.html.
5 Simone de Beauvoir, *The Coming of Age*, translated by P. O'Brian (New York: W. W. Norton, 1996), p. 4.
6 Ibid, p. 216.
7 James Hillman, *The Force of Character and the Lasting Life* (New York: Ballantine Books, 1999), p. 4.
8 William Irvine, *A Guide to the Good Life: The Ancient Art of Stoic Joy* (Oxford: Oxford University Press, 2009). pp. 192 and 194.
9 Beauvoir, *The Coming of Age*, p. 249.

10 Patrick Stokes and Adam Buben, "Editors' Introduction." In Patrick Stokes and Adam Buben (eds.), *Kierkegaard and Death* (Indianapolis: Indiana University Press, 2011), p. 2.

11 Søren Kierkegaard, *The Concept of Anxiety*, translated by W. Lowerie (Princeton, NJ: Princeton University Press, 1944), p. 55.

12 Søren Kierkegaard, *The Sickness unto Death*, translated by A. Hannay (New York: Penguin Books, 1989), p. 64, translation modified.

13 Ibid, p. 50.

14 Leo Tolstoy, *The Death of Ivan Ilych*, translated by A. Maude (New York: Signet Classics, 1960). p. 133.

15 Søren Kierkegaard, *Either/Or*, translated by D. Swenson, L. Swenson, and W. Lowrie. In Robert Bretall (ed.), *A Kierkegaard Anthology* (Princeton, NJ: Princeton University Press, 1973), p. 99.

16 Rainer Maria Rilke, *The Poet's Guide to Life*, translated by U. Baer (New York: Modern Library, 2005), p. 116.

17 Ibid, p. 112, translation modified.

18 Søren Kierkegaard, *Three Discourses on Imagined Occasions*, translated by E. Hong and H. Hong (Princeton, NJ: Princeton University Press, 1993), p. 96.

19 Søren Kierkegaard, *Fear and Trembling*, translated by W. Lowrie. In C. Guignon and D. Pereboom (eds.) *Existentialism: Basic Writings* (Indianapolis, IN: Hackett, 2001), pp. 44–45.

20 Kierkegaard, *Fear and Trembling*, p. 53.

21 Kierkegaard, *"The Moment" and Late Writings*, translated by H. Hong and E. Hong (Princeton, NJ: Princeton University Press, 1998), p. 177.

22 Martin Heidegger, *Being and Time*, translated by J. Macquarrie and E. Robinson (New York: Harper & Row, 1962), p. 358, translation modified.

23 Mary Pipher, *Women Rowing North: Navigating Life's Currents and Flourishing As We Age* (New York: Bloomsbury, 2019), p. 59.

24 Yalom, *Existential Psychotherapy*, p. 38.

25 Although the phrase "leap of faith" is attributed to Kierkegaard, it never appears in any of his published writings. The concept of the "leap," however, occurs many times.

26 Kierkegaard, *Fear and Trembling*, p. 47.

27 Yalom, *Existential Psychotherapy*, pp. 35–38.

28 Philip Bump, "A death every thirty-three seconds." *Washington Post*, December 19, 2020. https://www.wa shingtonpost.com/politics/2020/12/19/death-every-30-se conds.

29 B. J. Miller, "What is death?" *New York Times*, December 20, 2020. https://www.nytimes.com/2020/12/18/opinion /sunday/coronavirus-death.html.

30 Yalom, *Existential Psychotherapy*, p. 35.

31 Kierkegaard, *Fear and Trembling*, p. 47.

32 Ibid., p. 53.

33 John Leland, *Happiness Is a Choice You Make: Lessons from a Year among the Oldest Old* (New York: Sarah Crichton Books, 2018), p. 32.

34 Kierkegaard, *Three Discourses*, p. 76. Also cited in C. Guignon, "Heidegger and Kierkegaard on Death: The Existentiell and the Existential." In P. Stokes and A. Buben (eds.), *Kierkegaard and Death* (Indianapolis: Indiana University Press, 2011), pp. 184–203.

35 Kierkegaard, *Three Discourses*, p. 83.

Notes to Chapter 2

1 José Ortega y Gasset, *Toward a Philosophy of History*, translated by H. Weyl (New York: W. W. Norton, 1941), pp. 112, 201–202.

2 Ibid., p. 111.
3 Maurice Merleau-Ponty, *Phenomenology of Perception*, translated by C. Smith (New York: Routledge, 1962), pp. 453–454.
4 Jean-Paul Sartre, *Being and Nothingness*, translated by H. Barnes. In C. Guignon and D. Pereboom (eds.), *Existentialism: Basic Writings* (Indianapolis, IN: Hackett, 2001), p. 340.
5 Ibid., p. 90, translator's note.
6 Ibid., p. 88.
7 Jean-Paul Sartre, *The War Diaries*, translated by Q. Hoare. In N. Oaklander (ed.), *Existentialist Philosophy: An Introduction* (Upper Saddle River, NJ: Prentice Hall, 1996), p. 280.
8 Charles Guignon, *On Being Authentic* (London: Routledge, 2004), p. viii.
9 Miguel de Unamuno, *The Tragic Sense of Life*, translated by J. E. Crawford Flitch (New York: Dover Publications, 1954), p. 269, translation modified.
10 Friedrich Nietzsche, *Beyond Good and Evil*, translated by M. Faber (New York: Oxford University Press, 1998), p. 106.
11 James Hillman, *The Force of Character and the Lasting Life* (New York: Ballantine Books, 1999), p. 35.
12 Friedrich Nietzsche, *Ecce Homo: How One Becomes What One Is*, translated by W. Kaufmann (New York: Vintage Books, 1967), p. 9.
13 C. G. Jung, *Memories, Dreams, Reflections*, translated by R. and C. Winston (London: Collins & Routledge, 1963), p. 358.
14 Martin Heidegger, *Being and Time*, translated by J. Macquarrie and E. Robinson (New York: Harper & Row, 1962), pp. 347–369.
15 Ibid., p. 355.
16 Heidegger, *The Basic Problems of Phenomenology*, trans-

lated by A. Hofstadter (Bloomington: Indiana University Press, 1982), p. 376.

17 Heidegger, *Being and Time*, p. 187.

18 Ibid., 308.

19 Martin Heidegger, *Discourse on Thinking*, translated by J. Anderson and E. H. Freund (New York: Harper Torchbooks, 1966), p. 55.

20 Meister Eckhart, *The Complete Mystical Works*, translated by M. Walsche (New York: The Crossroad Publishing Company, 2009) p. 568, italics added.

21 John Leland, *Happiness Is a Choice You Make: Lessons from a Year among the Oldest Old* (New York: Sarah Crichton Books, 2018), p. 135.

22 Ibid., p. 137.

23 Ibid., p. 138.

24 Ibid., p. 137.

25 Rainer Maria Rilke, *The Poet's Guide to Life*, translated by U. Baer (New York: Modern Library, 2005), p. 115.

26 Laura Cartensen, "Social and Emotional Patterns in Adulthood: Support for Socioemotional Selectivity Theory," *Psychology and Aging* 7.3 (1992): 331–338.

27 Martin Heidegger, *The Concept of Time*, translated by W. McNeill (Oxford: Blackwell, 1992), p. 20, translation modified.

28 Heidegger, *Being and Time*, p. 185.

29 Heidegger, *The Concept of Time*, p. 14.

30 Heidegger, *Being and Time*, p. 216.

31 Quoted in Lawrence Samuel, *Aging in America: A Cultural History* (Philadelphia: University of Pennsylvania Press, 2017), p. 153.

32 Lillian B. Rubin, *Women of a Certain Age* (New York: Harper & Row, 1979), p. 123. Also quoted in Jeffrey Clair, David Karp, and William Yoels, *Experiencing the Life Cycle: A Social Psychology of Aging* (Springfield, IL: Thomas Books, 1993), p. 105.

33 Irvin Yalom, *Staring at the Sun: Overcoming the Terror of Death*. San Francisco, CA: Jossey-Bass, 2008).
34 Ibid., pp. 167 and 209.

Notes to Chapter 3

1 Simone de Beauvoir, *The Coming of Age*, translated by P. O'Brian (New York: W. W. Norton, 1996), p. 461.
2 Ibid.
3 Martin Heidegger, *Being and Time*, translated by J. Macquarrie and E. Robinson (New York: Harper & Row, 1962), p. 164.
4 Martin Heidegger, *Contributions to Philosophy (From Enowning)*, translated by P. Emad and K. Maly (Bloomington: Indiana University Press, 1999), p. 84.
5 Martin Heidegger, *Fundamental Concepts of Metaphysics: World, Finitude, Solitude*, translated by W. McNeill and N. Walker (Bloomington: Indiana University Press, 1995) p. 128.
6 Blaise Pascal, *Pensées*, translated by A. J. Krailsheimer (New York: Penguin Classics, 1966) p. 120.
7 Ibid., pp. 39–40.
8 Ibid., p. 208.
9 Ibid., p. 40.
10 Ibid., p. 208.
11 Heidegger, *Contributions to Philosophy*, p. 84.
12 Heidegger, *Fundamental Concepts of Metaphysics*, p. 126.
13 Ibid.
14 Martin Heidegger, "Meßkirch's Seventh Centennial," translated by T. Sheehan. *Listening* 8.1–3 (1973), pp. 40–57, here pp. 50–51.
15 Marco van Leeuwen, "The Digital Void: E-NNUI and Experience." In B. Pezze and C. Salzani (eds.), *Essays on Boredom and Modernity* (New York: Rodopi Press, 2009), p. 188.

16 Søren Kierkegaard, *Either/Or*, translated by H. Hong and E. Hong (Princeton, NJ: Princeton University Press, 1987), p. 291.

17 Kierkegaard, *Works of Love*, translated by H. Hong and E. Hong (Princeton, NJ: Princeton University Press, 1995), p. 98.

18 Ibid., 247.

19 Kierkegaard, *Either/Or*, p. 291, translation modified.

20 Ibid., p. 290.

21 Ibid., p. 289.

22 Baba Ram Dass, *Still Here: Embracing Aging, Changing, and Dying* (New York: Riverside Books, 2001), p. 39.

23 Kierkegaard, *Either/Or*, p. 293.

24 Martin Buber, *Eclipse of God: Studies in the Relation between Religion and Philosophy* (Princeton, NJ: Princeton University Press, 2016), p. 4.

25 Martin Heidegger, *Discourse on Thinking*, translated by J. Anderson and E. H. Freund (New York: Harper Torchbooks, 1966), p. 47.

26 Martin Heidegger, *Elucidations of Hölderlin's Poetry*, translated by K. Hoeller (Amherst, NY: Humanity Books, 2000), p. 153, my emphasis.

27 Martin Heidegger, *Basic Questions of Philosophy: Selected Problems of Logic*, translated by R. Rojcewicz and A. Schuwer (Bloomington: Indiana University Press, 1994), p. 150.

28 Stephen Batchelor, *Buddhism without Beliefs: A Contemporary Guide to Awakening* (New York: Riverhead Books, 1997), p. 21.

29 Ibid., p. 67.

30 Heidegger, *Discourse on Thinking*, p. 56.

31 Gabriel Marcel, *Being and Having*, translated by K. Farrer (Glasgow: Glasgow University Press, 1949), p. 166.

32 Gabriel Marcel, *Homo Viator: Introduction to a*

Metaphysics of Hope, translated by E. Craufurd (Chicago, IL: Henry Regnery Company, 1951), p. 61.

33 Marcel, *Being and Having*, p. 175.

34 Marcel, *Homo Viator*, p. 62.

35 Stephen Batchelor, *Alone with Others: An Existential Approach to Buddhism* (New York: Grove Press, 1983), pp. 36–37.

36 Friedrich Nietzsche, *The Gay Science*, translated by W. Kaufman (New York: Random House, 1974), p. 259.

37 Ibid.

38 Friedrich Nietzsche, *Human, All Too Human: A Book for Free Spirits*, translated by R. J. Hollingdale (Cambridge: Cambridge University Press, 1996), aphorisms 282 and 285.

39 Nietzsche, *The Gay Science*, p. 259.

40 Nietzsche, as quoted in Rüdiger Safranski, *Nietzsche: A Philosophical Biography* (New York: W. W. Norton, 2002), p. 105. The quotation is from "Wagner in Untimely Meditations," the last in a series of four pieces titled *Unzeitgemässe Betrachtungen* (known in English as *Untimely Meditations* or *Observations and Thoughts out of Season*).

41 Friedrich Nietzsche, *Thus Spoke Zarathustra: A Book for None and All*, translated by W. Kaufman (New York: Penguin Books, 1978), p. 51.

42 Ibid., p. 277.

43 Ibid., p. 276.

44 Nietzsche, as quoted in Roslyn Jolly, "In the Footsteps of Friedrich Nietzsche." *Intrepid Times*, November 14, 2018. https://intrepidtimes.com/2018/11/in-the-footsteps-of-friedrich-nietzsche.

45 From Nietzsche's poem "Sils Maria," quoted here from Joan Stambaugh, "Heidegger, Taoism, and Metaphysics." In Graham Parkes (ed.), *Heidegger and Asian Thought*

(Honolulu, HI: University of Hawaii Press, 1987), p. 86.

46 Nietzsche, *Thus Spoke Zarathustra*, p. 300.

Notes to Chapter 4

1 Martin Heidegger, *Nietzsche*, vol. 1, translated by D. F. Krell (New York: Harper & Row, 1979), p. 99. Here I am indebted to John Kaag, "How to Live with Dying." *American Scholar*, September 30, 2021.

2 Gabriel Marcel, *Mystery of Being: Reflection and Mystery*, vol. 1 (South Bend, IN: Gateway Editions, 1951), p. 104.

3 Maurice Merleau-Ponty, *Phenomenology of Perception*, translated by C. Smith (New York: Routledge, 1962), p. 137.

4 Ibid., p. x.

5 Simone de Beauvoir, *The Force of Circumstance*, vol. 2: *Hard Times, 1952–1962*, translated by R. Howard (New York: Paragon House, 1992), p. 375.

6 Ibid., p. 379, emphasis added.

7 Simone de Beauvoir, *The Coming of Age*, translated by P. O'Brian (New York: W. W. Norton, 1996), p. 303.

8 Ibid., p. 304.

9 Ibid., p. 443. Here I am indebted to Sonia Kruks, *Simone de Beauvoir and the Politics of Ambiguity* (Oxford: Oxford University Press, 2012), pp. 81–89.

10 Beauvoir, *The Force of Circumstance*, vol. 2, p. 378.

11 Ibid., pp. 376 and 378.

12 Simone de Beauvoir, *The Second Sex*, translated by H. M. Parshley (New York: Vintage Books, 1989), p. 337.

13 Beauvoir, *The Force of Circumstance*, vol. 2, p. 7.

14 Beauvoir, *The Coming of Age*, p. 123, translation modified.

15 Mary Pipher, *Women Rowing North: Navigating Life's*

Currents and Flourishing As We Age (New York: Bloomsbury, 2019), p. 32.

16 Dwight Garner, "Cataloging the insults (and joys) of old age." *New York Times*, January 13, 2009. https://www.nytimes.com/2009/01/14/books/14garn.html?searchResultPosition=1.

17 Quoted in Lawrence Samuel, *Aging in America: A Cultural History* (Philadelphia: University of Pennsylvania Press, 2017), p. 156.

18 Martha Nussbaum and Saul Levmore, *Aging Thoughtfully: Conversations about Retirement, Romance, Wrinkles, and Regret* (Oxford: Oxford University Press, 2017), p. 20.

19 Beauvoir, *The Force of Circumstance*, vol. 2, p. 377.

20 See Shannon Musset, "Ageing and Existentialism: Simone de Beauvoir and the Limits of Freedom." In C. Tandy (ed.), *Death and Anti-Death*, vol. 4: *Twenty Years after Beauvoir and Thirty Years after Heidegger* (Palo Alto, CA: Ria University Press, 2006), pp. 231–255.

21 Sharon Olds, *Odes* (New York: Alfred A. Knopf, 2016), p. 78.

22 Ibid., pp. 82–83.

23 Beauvoir, *The Force of Circumstance*, vol. 2, pp. 378–379.

24 Olds, *Odes*, p. 27.

25 Simone de Beauvoir, *All Said and Done: The Autobiography of Simone de Beauvoir, 1962–1972*, translated by R. Howard (New York: Paragon Press, 1994), pp. 75–76. See Toril Moi, *Simone de Beauvoir: The Making of an Intellectual Woman* (Oxford: Oxford University Press, 2008), p. 260.

26 Beauvoir, *The Coming of Age*, p. 540.

27 Beauvoir, *The Force of Circumstance*, vol. 2, pp. 373–374.

28 Beauvoir, *The Coming of Age*, p. 6.

29 Ibid., p. 543.

30 Ibid.
31 Ibid., p. 248.
32 Oliver Sacks, *Gratitude* (New York: Alfred A. Knopf, 2019), pp. 10–11.
33 Ibid., p. 18.
34 Ibid., pp. 16 and 20.

Notes to Chapter 5

1 Nietzsche, *The Gay Science*, translated by W. Kaufmann (New York: Vintage, 1974), section 374.
2 Charles Guignon, *On Being Authentic* (London: Routledge, 2004), p. 127.
3 Nietzsche, *The Gay Science*, section 274.
4 Kevin Aho, *Existentialism* (2nd edn., Cambridge: Polity, 2020), pp. 60–63.
5 Irvin Yalom and Marilyn Yalom, *A Matter of Death and Life* (Stanford, CA: Stanford University Press, 2021), p. 70.
6 Friedrich Nietzsche, *On the Genealogy of Morals*, translated by D. Smith (Oxford: Oxford University Press, 1996), p. 24. Nietzsche is referring to Honoré Gabriel Riqueti, Count of Mirabeau, an important figure in the French Revolution. I am thankful to Gordon Marino's work for bringing this passage to my attention.
7 Ibid.
8 Laura Carstensen and Mara Mather, "Aging and Motivated Cognition: The Positivity Effect in Attention and Memory." *Trends in Cognitive Science* 9 (2005): 496–502.
9 Elizabeth Barry, "Critical Interests and Critical Endings: Dementia, Personhood and the End of Life in Matthew Thomas's *We Are not Ourselves*." In E. Barry and M. V. Skagen (eds.), *Literature and Ageing* (Cambridge: D. S. Brewer, 2020), pp. 129–148, here p. 130.

10 Heidegger, "On the Essence of Ground," in Martin Heidegger, *Pathmarks*, translated by W. McNeill (Cambridge: Cambridge University Press, 1998), p. 108, translation modified.

11 Of all the existentialists, Sartre is the only one to whom this hard reading can be attributed, namely in his earlier writings (esp. *Being and Nothingness*); see also his conception of "subjectivity" and of an unconditioned "freedom in consciousness," a view he later rejects for being overly Cartesian.

12 Maurice Merleau-Ponty, *The Visible and the Invisible*, translated by A. Lingis (Evanston, IL: Northwestern University Press, 1968), p. 5.

13 Friedrich Nietzsche, *Thus Spoke Zarathustra: A Book for None and All*, translated by W. Kaufmann (New York: Penguin Books, 1978), pp. 34–35, emphasis added.

14 See Marie Marley, *Come Back Early Today: A Memoir of Love, Alzheimer's and Joy* (Olathe, KS: Joseph Peterson Books, 2011).

15 Yalom and Yalom, *A Matter of Death and Life*, p. 71.

16 Jill Chonody and Barbra Teater, *Social Work Practice with Older Adults: An Actively Aging Framework for Practice* (London: Sage, 2018), p. 34.

17 Charles Taylor, *Sources of the Self: The Making of the Modern Identity* (Cambridge, MA: Harvard University Press, 1989), p. 47.

18 Simone de Beauvoir, *The Coming of Age*, translated by P. O'Brian (New York: W. W. Norton, 1996), p. 283.

19 Ibid.

20 Ibid., p. 362.

21 Ibid.

22 Hanne Laceulle and Jan Baars, "Self-Realization and Cultural Narratives about Later Life." *Journal of Aging Studies* 31 (2014): 34–44.

23 Hanne Laceulle writes: "Decline narratives suggest that

such vulnerability should be passively and patiently endured because it is an inevitable reality of life. Age-defying narratives take the opposite position and imply that efforts should be made to actively resist the reality of existential vulnerability for as long as possible" (Hanne Laceulle, "Aging and the Ethics of Authenticity." *Gerontologist* 58.5 (2018), p. 971).

24 Albert Camus, *The Rebel*, translated by E. Bower (New York: Vintage Books, 1956), p. 13.

25 Ibid., pp. 13–14.

26 Ibid., pp. 14–15.

27 Ibid., p. 22.

28 Martin Heidegger, *Being and Time*, translated by J. Macquarrie and E. Robinson (New York: Harper & Row, 1962), p. 129.

29 Martin Heidegger, *The Question Concerning Technology and Other Essays*, translated by W. Lovitt (New York: Harper Torchbooks, 1977), p. 27.

30 Martin Heidegger, *Plato's Sophist*, translated by R. Rojcewicz and A. Schuwer (Bloomington: Indiana University Press, 1997), p. 7.

31 Heidegger, *Being and Time*, p. 425.

32 Drew Leder, "What Is It to 'Age Well'? Re-Visioning Later Life." In K. Aho (ed.), *Existential Medicine: Essays on Health and Illness* (London: Rowman & Littlefield, 2018), pp. 226–233.

33 Friedrich Nietzsche, *The Will to Power*, translated by W. Kaufmann (New York: Vintage Books, 1968), pp. 377–378.

34 Martin Heidegger, "The Origin of the Work of Art," translated by A. Hofstadter. In *Martin Heidegger: Basic Writings* (New York: HarperCollins, 1993), pp. 188–189.

35 Guignon, *On Being Authentic*, p. 129.

36 Alexander Nehamas, *Nietzsche: Life as Literature* (Cambridge, MA: Harvard University Press, 1985).

37 Nietzsche, *The Gay Science*, section 290.
38 Nietzsche, *The Will to Power*, pp. 270–271.
39 Nietzsche, *The Gay Science*, section 144.
40 Nietzsche, *Thus Spoke Zarathustra*, p. 195.
41 Ibid., p. 193.
42 Friedrich Nietzsche, *Beyond Good and Evil*, translated by M. Fabor (Oxford: Oxford University Press, 1998), p. 31.
43 Nietzsche, *The Gay Science*, section 299.
44 Nietzsche, *The Will to Power*, p. 536.
45 John Leland, *Happiness Is a Choice You Make: Lessons from a Year among the Oldest Old* (New York: Sarah Crichton Books, 2018), p. 210.
46 Nietzsche, *Thus Spoke Zarathustra*, p. 318.

Notes to Chapter 6

1 Erich Fromm, *The Art of Loving* (New York: Bantam Books, 1956), p. 7.
2 Irvin Yalom, *Existential Psychotherapy* (New York: Basic Books, 1980), p. 353.
3 Tara John, "How the world's first loneliness minster will tackle the 'sad reality of modern life.'" *Time*, April 25, 2018. https://time.com/5248016/tracey-crouch-uk-loneliness-minister.
4 Kevin Aho, "The Uncanny in the Time of Pandemics: Heideggerian Reflections on the Coronavirus," *Gatherings: The Heidegger Circle Annual* 10 (2020): 1–19.
5 Paula Span, "Just what older people didn't need: More isolation." *New York Times*, April 13, 2020. https://www.nytimes.com/2020/04/13/health/coronavirus-elderly-isolation-loneliness.html.
6 Martin Heidegger, *Pathmarks*, translated by W. McNeill (Cambridge: Cambridge University Press, 1998), p. 88.
7 Hannah Arendt, *The Origins of Totalitarianism* (New York: Meridian Books, 1958), p. 475.

8 Ibid., p. 475.

9 Ibid., p. 478.

10 Ibid.

11 Ibid., p. 477.

12 Ibid., p. 475.

13 Yalom, *Existential Psychotherapy*, p. 374.

14 Jean-Paul Sartre, *Being and Nothingness*, translated by H. Barnes. In C. Guignon and D. Pereboom (eds.), *Existentialism: Basic Writings* (Indianapolis, IN: Hackett, 2001), p. 475.

15 Yalom, *Existential Psychotherapy*, p. 378.

16 Ibid., p. 380.

17 Søren Kierkegaard, *Either/Or*, translated by D. Swenson, L. Swenson, and W. Lowrie. In R. Bretall (ed.), *A Kierkegaard Anthology* (Princeton, NJ: Princeton University Press, 1973), pp. 29–30.

18 Yalom, *Existential Psychotherapy*, p. 383.

19 Kierkegaard, *Either/Or*, p. 83.

20 Ibid., 76.

21 Kevin Aho, "Kierkegaard on Boredom and Self-Loss in the Age of Online Dating." In M. Gardner and J. J. Haladyn (eds.), *The Boredom Studies Reader: Frameworks and Perspectives* (London: Routledge, 2016).

22 Sigmund Freud, *The Freud Reader*, edited by Peter Gay (New York: W. W. Norton, 1989), p. 72.

23 Friedrich Nietzsche, *The Twilight of the Idols*, translated by R. J. Hollingdale (New York: Penguin Classics, 1990), p. 170.

24 Ibid., pp. 62 and 64.

25 Friedrich Nietzsche, "On Truth and Lies in a Nonmoral Sense." In Friedrich Nietzsche, *Philosophy and Truth: Selections from Nietzsche's Notebooks of the Early 1870s*, translated by D. Breazeale (Atlantic Highlands, NJ: Humanities Press, 1990), pp. 79–100, here p. 84.

26 Friedrich Nietzsche, *The Gay Science*, translated by

W. Kaufman (New York: Random House, 1974), aphorism 125.

27 Paul Tillich, "Let Us Dare to Have Solitude." *Union Seminary Quarterly Review* 13 (1957): 9, translation modified.

28 Mick Cooper, *Existential Therapies* (London: Sage, 2003), p. 82.

29 Sarah Barber, Philip Opitz, Bruna Martins, Michiko Sakaki, and Mara Mather, "Thinking about a Limited Future Enhances the Positivity of Younger and Older Adults' Recall: Support for Socioemotional Selectivity Theory." *Memory and Cognition* 44.6 (2016): 869–882.

30 Susan Krauss and Joel Sneed, "The Paradox of Well-Being, Identity Processes, and Stereotype Threat: Ageism and Its Potential Relationship to the Self in Later Life." In T. Nelson (ed.), *Ageism: Stereotyping and Prejudice against Older Persons* (Cambridge, MA: MIT Press, 2007).

31 Martin Buber, *I and Thou*, translated by W. Kaufmann (New York: Touchstone, 1970), pp. 75 and 125.

32 Ibid., p. 85.

33 Ibid., p. 60.

34 Ibid., p. 63.

35 Ibid., p. 60.

36 Ibid., p. 95.

37 Martin Buber, *Between Man and Man*, translated by R. Gregor Smith (New York: Macmillan, 1965), p. 11.

38 Yalom, *Existential Psychotherapy*, p. 398.

39 Buber, *I and Thou*, p. 70.

40 Ibid., p. 125.

41 Maurice Friedman, *Martin Buber's Life and Work: The Later Years, 1945–1965* (New York: E. P. Dutton, 1983), p. 408.

42 Ibid.

43 Maurice Friedman, *Martin Buber and the Human Sciences* (Albany, NY: SUNY Press, 1996), p. 4.
44 Buber, *I and Thou*, p. 63.
45 Ibid., p. 85.
46 Friedman, *Martin Buber's Life and Work*, p. 414.
47 Ibid., p. 416.
48 Martin Heidegger, *Being and Time*, translated by J. Macquarrie and E. Robinson (New York: Harper & Row, 1962), p. 222.
49 Buber, *I and Thou*, p. 143.

Notes to Chapter 7

1 Walter Kaufmann, "Translator's Preface." In Friedrich Nietzsche, *Thus Spoke Zarathustra* (New York: Penguin Books, 1978), pp. xiii–xiv.
2 Nietzsche, as quoted in Rüdiger Safranski, *Nietzsche: A Philosophical Biography*, translated by S. Frisch (New York: W. W. Norton, 2002), p. 306.
3 Nietzsche, as quoted in Rüdiger Safranski, *Nietzsche: A Philosophical Biography*, translated by S. Frisch (New York: W. W. Norton, 2002), p. 314. The quotation comes from Nietzsche's correspondence.
4 Friedrich Nietzsche, *Ecce Homo*, translated by Walter Kaufmann (New York: Vintage Books, 1989), p. 255, translation modified.
5 Ibid., p. 221.
6 See Sara Algoe, Shelly Gable, and Natalya Maisel, "It's the Little Things: Everyday Gratitude as a Booster Shot for Romantic Relationships." *Journal of Theoretical Social Psychology* 17.2 (2010): 217–233; Alex Wood, Stephen Joseph, Joanna Lloyd, and Samuel Atkins, "Gratitude Influences Sleep through the Mechanism of Pre-Sleep Cognitions." *Journal of Psychosomatic Research* 66.1 (2009): 43–48; Eshter Frinking, Lilian Jans-Beken, Mayke

Janssens, Sanne Peeters, Johan Lataster, Nele Jacobs, and Jennifer Reijnders, "Gratitude and Loneliness in Adults over 40 Years: Examining the Role of Psychological Flexibility and Engaged Living." *Aging and Mental Health* 24.12 (2020): 2117–2124.

7 Lakeshia Cousin, Laura Redwine, Christina Bricker, Kevin Kip, and Harleah Buck, "Effect of Gratitude on Cardiovascular Health Outcomes: A State of the Science Review." *Journal of Positive Psychology* 16.3 (2021): 348–355.

8 William Chopik, Nicky Newton, Lindsay Ryan, Todd Kashdan, and Aaron Jarden,,"Gratitude Across the Life Span: Age Differences and Links to Subjective Well-Being." *Journal of Positive Psychology* 14.3 (2020): 292–302.

9 Mary Pipher, *Women Rowing North: Navigating Life's Currents and Flourishing As We Age* (New York: Bloomsbury, 2019), p. 162. Cf. Polly Young-Eisendrath, *The Resilient Spirit: Transforming Suffering into Insight and Renewal* (New York: Addison-Wesley Publishing, 1996).

10 John Leland, *Happiness Is a Choice You Make: Lessons from a Year among the Oldest Old* (New York: Sarah Crichton Books, 2018), p. 110.

11 Ibid., p. 111.

12 Robert Solomon, "Foreword." In R. Emmons and M. McCullough (eds.), *The Psychology of Gratitude* (Oxford: Oxford University Press, 2004), pp. viii–ix.

13 Friedrich Nietzsche, *On the Genealogy of Morals*, translated by D. Smith (Oxford: Oxford University Press, 1998), p. 12.

14 Rainer Maria Rilke, *The Poet's Guide to Life*, translated by U. Baer (New York: Modern Library, 2005) p. 120.

15 Friedrich Nietzsche, *The Gay Science*, translated by Richard Polt. In C. Guignon and D. Pereboom (eds.),

Existentialism: Basic Writings (Indianapolis, IN: Hackett, 2001), pp. 147–148.

16 Nietzsche, as quoted in Rüdiger Safranski, *Nietzsche: A Philosophical Biography*, translated by S. Frisch (New York: W. W. Norton, 2002), p. 306.

17 Ibid., p. 148.

18 Jody Gastfriend, "Want to enjoy old age? This 90-year-old has one simple trick, and science backs her up." *Forbes*, November 28, 2018. https://www.forbes.com/sites/jodyg astfriend/2018/11/20/gratitude-and-enjoying-old-age/?sh =35a0e0885d78.

19 Nietzsche, *The Gay Science*, p. 170.

20 Ibid., pp. 142–143.

21 Nietzsche was deeply moved after discovering Dostoevsky's work through a French copy of *Notes from the Underground* (*L'esprit souterrain*), which he found in a bookshop in Nice in the winter of 1886/1887. He described him as a "bracing and incisive kindred spirit"—as quoted in Jeff Love and Jeffrey Metzger (eds.), *Nietzsche and Dostoevsky: Philosophy, Morality, Tragedy* (Evanston, IL: Northwestern University Press, 2016), p. xiv.

22 Fyodor Dostoevsky, *Notes from the Underground*, translated by C. Garnett (Cambridge, MA: Hackett, 2004), p. 22.

23 For this interpretation I am especially indebted to Deborah Martinsen, "Ingratitude and the Underground." *Dostoevsky Studies* (New Series) 17 (2013): 7–12.

24 Dostoevsky, *Notes from the Underground*, p. 20.

25 Kevin Aho, *Existentialism* (2nd edn., Cambridge: Polity, 2020), pp. 71–75.

26 Kevin Aho, "Dostoevsky, Existential Therapy, and Modern Rage: On the Possibility of Counseling the Underground Man." *Journal of Humanistic Psychology* 61.5 (2019): 828–845. doi: 10.1177/0022167819852234.

27 Dostoevsky, *Notes from the Underground*, pp. 89–90.
28 Ibid., p. 1.
29 Fyodor Dostoevsky, *The Brothers Karamazov*, translated by C. Garnett (New York: Signet Classics, 1980), p. 276.
30 Ibid., p. 289.
31 Ibid.
32 Charles Guignon, "Editor's Introduction." In Fyodor Dostoevsky, *Dostoevsky's Grand Inquisitor, with Related Chapters for The Brothers Karamazov* (Indianapolis, IN: Hackett, 1993), p. xxxvii.
33 Dostoevsky, *The Brothers Karamazov*, p. 288.
34 Ibid., p. 289.
35 Joseph Davis, "The Devalued Status of Old Age." In J. Davis and P. Scherz (eds.), *The Evening of Life: The Challenges of Aging and Dying Well* (South Bend, IN: Notre Dame University Press, 2020), p. 28.
36 Cf. Linda Ivanitis, *Dostoevsky and the Russian People* (Cambridge: Cambridge University Press, 2008).
37 Fyodor Dostoevsky, *Crime and Punishment*, translated by R. Pevear and L. Volokhonsky (New York: Vintage Classics, 1993), pp. 332–333.
38 Without this theme of redemption, *Notes from the Underground* is perhaps the most anti-Dostoevskyian of all of Dostoevsky's great works. Censors deleted what he called the "essential idea" of his story in the penultimate chapter of the *Notes*, an idea that affirms the "necessity of faith in Christ." Their changes were frustrating to Dostoevsky, but he accepted them because he was constantly short of money and unwilling to delay publication. See *Selected Letters of Fyodor Dostoevsky*, translated by A. MacAndrew (London: Routledge, 1989), p. 191.
39 Ivanitis, *Dostoevsky and the Russian People*, pp. 176–177.

40 Dostoevsky, *Notes from the Underground*, p. 93.
41 Dostoevsky, *The Brothers Karamazov*, p. 290.

Notes to Chapter 8

1 Leo Tolstoy, *The Death of Ivan Ilych*, translated by A. Maude (New York: Signet Classics, 1960), p. 137.
2 Atul Gawande, *Being Mortal: Medicine and What Matters in the End* (New York: Henry Holt, 2014), p. 6.
3 Susan Wendell, *The Rejected Body: Feminist Philosophical Reflections on Disability* (London: Routledge, 1996), p. 96.
4 Kevin Aho, "Gadamer and Health." In T. George and G-J van der Heiden (eds.), *The Gadamerian Mind* (London: Routledge, 2021), p. 184.
5 Gawande, *Being Mortal*, p. 28.
6 Hans Georg-Gadamer, *The Enigma of Health: The Art of Healing in the Scientific Age*, translated by J. Gaiger and N. Walker (Stanford, CA: Stanford University Press, 1996), p. 62.
7 Tolstoy, *The Death of Ivan Ilych*, p. 138.
8 Ibid.
9 Ibid., p. 172.
10 B. J. Miller, "What is death?," *New York Times*, December 20, 2020.
11 Friedrich Nietzsche, *Twilight of the Idols and The Anti-Christ*, translated by R. J. Hollingdale (New York: Penguin Books, 1990), p. 99.
12 Gawande, *Being Mortal*, p. 243.
13 Ibid.
14 Ibid., p. 259.
15 Jean-Paul Sartre, "The Humanism of Existentialism." In C. Guigon and D. Pereboom (eds.), *Existentialism: Basic Writings* (Indianapolis, IN: Hackett Press, 2001), p. 293.
16 Tolstoy, *The Death of Ivan Ilych*, p. 104.

17 Ibid., p. 148, translation modified.
18 Ibid., p. 155.
19 Ibid., p. 156.
20 Patrick Olivelle, *The Ashrama System: The History and Hermeneutics of a Religious Institution* (Oxford: Oxford University Press, 1993), p. 3.
21 Cf. Arthur Brooks, "Your professional decline is coming (much) sooner than you think." *The Atlantic*, July 2019.
22 Olivelle, *The Ashrama System*, p. 121.
23 Jacques Maritain and Raïssa Maritain, *The Situation of Poetry*, translated by M. Suther (Berkeley, CA: Philosophical Library, 1955), p. 46.
24 Rainer Maria Rilke, *The Dark Interval: Letters on Loss, Grief, and Transformation*, translated by U. Baer (New York: Modern Library, 2018), p. 64.
25 Ibid., p. 3.
26 Rainer Maria Rilke, *The Book of Hours: Love Poems to God*, translated by A. Barrows and J. Macy (New York: Riverhead Books, 2005), p. 87.
27 Martin Heidegger, *Being and Time*, translated by J. Macquarrie and E. Robinson (New York: Harper & Row, 1962), p. 367.
28 Martin Heidegger, "What Is Metaphysics?," translated by J. Sallis. In M. Heidegger, *Basic Writings* (New York: HarperCollins, 1993), p. 100.
29 Martin Heidegger, "On the Essence of Truth," translated by J. Sallis. In M. Heidegger, *Basic Writings* (New York: HarperCollins, 1993) p. 125.
30 Ibid.
31 Heidegger, *Being and Time*, p. 251.
32 Heidegger, "What Is Metaphysics?," p. 110.
33 Heidegger, as quoted in Julian Young, *Heidegger's Later Philosophy* (New York: Cambridge University Press, 2000), p. 60, italics added. (The quotation is from a piece titled "Hölderlin's Hymn '*Andenken*.'")

34 Riitta-Liisa Heikkinen, "The Experience of Aging and Advanced Old Age: A Ten-Year Follow Up," *Aging & Society* 24 (2004): 567–582.

35 Ibid., p. 576.

36 Ibid.

37 Ibid., p. 579.

38 Martin Heidegger, *Basic Questions of Philosophy: Selected Problems of Logic*, translated by R. Rojcewicz and A. Schuwer (Bloomington: Indiana University Press, 1994), p. 151.

39 Oliver Sacks, *Gratitude* (New York: Alfred A. Knopf, 2019), p. 18.

40 Ibid., pp. 11 and 18.

41 Martin Heidegger, *What Is Called Thinking?*, translated by J. Glenn Gray (New York: Harper & Row, 1968).

42 Martin Heidegger, *Discourse on Thinking*, translated by J. Anderson and E. H. Freund (New York: Harper Torchbooks, 1966), p. 55.

43 Heidegger, *What Is Called Thinking?*, p. 31.

44 Sacks, *Gratitude*, p. 20.

Bibliography

Aho, Kevin. "Dostoevsky, Existential Therapy, and Modern Rage." *Journal of Humanistic Psychology*, 61.5 (2019): 828–845.

Aho, Kevin. *Existentialism* (2nd edn., Cambridge: Polity, 2020).

Aho, Kevin. "Gadamer and Health." In T. George and G.-J. van der Heiden (eds.), *The Gadamerian Mind*, pp. 177–187 (London: Routledge, 2021).

Aho, Kevin. "Kierkegaard on Boredom and Self-Loss in the Age of Online Dating." In M. Gardner and J. J. Haladyn (eds.), *The Boredom Studies Reader: Frameworks and Perspectives*, pp. 130–142 (London: Routledge, 2016).

Aho, Kevin. "The Uncanny in the Time of Pandemics: Heideggerian Reflections on the Coronavirus." *Gatherings: The Heidegger Circle Annual*, 10 (2020): 1–19.

Algoe, Sarah, Gable, Shelly, and Maisel, Natalya. "It's the Little Things: Everyday Gratitude as a Booster Shot for Romantic Relationships." *Journal of Theoretical Social Psychology* 17.2 (2010): 217–233.

Bibliography

Arendt, Hannah. *The Origins of Totalitarianism* (New York: Meridian Books, 1958).

Barber, Sarah, Opitz, Philip, Martins, Bruna, Sakaki, Michiko, and Mather, Mara. "Thinking about a Limited Future Enhances the Positivity of Younger and Older Adults' Recall: Support for Socioemotional Selectivity Theory." *Memory and Cognition* 44.6 (2016): 869–882.

Barry, Elizabeth. "Critical Interests and Critical Endings: Dementia, Personhood and the End of Life in Matthew Thomas's *We Are not Ourselves*." In E. Barry and M. V. Skagen (eds.), *Literature and Ageing*, pp. 129–148 (Cambridge: D. S. Brewer, 2020).

Batchelor, Stephen. *Alone with Others: An Existential Approach to Buddhism* (New York: Grove Press, 1983).

Batchelor, Stephen. *Buddhism without Beliefs: A Contemporary Guide to Awakening* (New York: Riverhead Books, 1997).

Beauvoir, Simone de. *All Said and Done: The Autobiography of Simone de Beauvoir, 1962–1972*, translated by R. Howard (New York: Paragon Press, 1994).

Beauvoir, Simone de. *The Coming of Age*, translated by P. O'Brian (New York: W. W. Norton, 1996).

Beauvoir, Simone de. *The Force of Circumstance*, vol. 2: *Hard Times, 1952–1962*, translated by R. Howard (New York: Paragon House, 1992).

Beauvoir, Simone de. *The Second Sex*, translated by H. M. Parshley (New York: Vintage Books, 1989).

Buber, Martin. *Between Man and Man*, translated by R. Gregor Smith (New York: Macmillan, 1965).

Bibliography

Buber, Martin. *Eclipse of God: Studies in the Relation between Religion and Philosophy* (Princeton, NJ: Princeton University Press, 2016).

Buber, Martin. *I and Thou*, translated by W. Kaufman (New York: Touchstone, 1970).

Camus, Albert. *The Rebel*, translated by A. Bower (New York: Vintage Books, 1956).

Caputo, John. *The Mystical Element in Heidegger's Thought* (New York: Fordham University Press, 1986).

Cartensen, Laura. "Social and Emotional Patterns in Adulthood: Support for Socioemotional Selectivity Theory." *Psychology and Aging* 7.3 (1992): 331–338.

Cartensen, Laura and Mather, Mara. "Aging and Motivated Cognition: The Positivity Effect in Attention and Memory." *Trends in Cognitive Science* 9 (2005): 469–502.

Chonody, Jill and Teater, Barbra. *Social Work Practice with Older Adults: An Actively Aging Framework for Practice* (London: Sage, 2018).

Chopik, William, Newton, Nicky, Ryan, Lindsay, Kashdan, Todd, and Jarden, Aaron. "Gratitude across the Life Span: Age Differences and Links to Subjective Well-Being." *Journal of Positive Psychology* 14.3 (2020): 292–302.

Clair, Jeffrey, Karp, David, and Yoels, William. *Experiencing the Life Cycle: A Social Psychology of Aging* (Springfield, IL: Thomas Books, 1993).

Cooper, Mick. *Existential Therapies* (London: Sage, 2003).

Cousin, Lakeshia, Redwine, Laura, Bricker, Christina, Kip, Kevin, and Buck, Harleah. "Effect of Gratitude on Cardiovascular Health Outcomes: A State of the

Science Review." *Journal of Positive Psychology* 16.3 (2021): 348–355.

Davis, Joseph. "The Devalued Status of Old Age." In J. Davis and P. Scherz (eds.), *The Evening of Life: The Challenges of Aging and Dying Well*, pp. 23–37 (South Bend, IN: Notre Dame University Press, 2020).

Dostoevsky, Fyodor. *The Brothers Karamazov*, translated by C. Garnett (New York: Signet Classics, 1980).

Dostoevsky, Fyodor. *Crime and Punishment*, translated by R. Pevear and L. Volokhonsky (New York: Vintage Classics, 1993).

Dostoevsky, Fyodor. *Notes from the Underground*, translated by C. Garnett (Cambridge, MA: Hackett, 2004).

Dostoevsky, Fyodor. *Selected Letters of Fyodor Dostoevsky*, translated by A. MacAndrew (London: Routledge, 1989).

Eckhart, Meister. *The Complete Mystical Works*, translated by M. Walsche (New York: The Crossroads Publishing Company, 2009).

Freud, Sigmund. *The Freud Reader*, edited by Peter Gay (New York: W. W. Norton, 1989).

Friedman, Maurice. *Martin Buber and the Human Sciences* (Albany, NY: SUNY Press, 1996).

Friedman, Maurice. *Martin Buber's Life and Work: The Later Years, 1945–1965* (New York: E. P. Dutton, 1983).

Fromm, Erich. *The Art of Loving* (New York: Bantam Books, 1956).

Frinking, Esther, Jans-Beken, Lilian, Janssens, Mayke, Peeters, Sanne, Lataster, Johan, Jacobs, Nele, and Reijnders, Jennifer. "Gratitude and Loneliness in Adults over 40 Years: Examining the Role of

Psychological Flexibility and Engaged Living." *Aging and Mental Health* 24.12 (2020): 2117–2124.

Gadamer, Hans-Georg. *The Enigma of Health: The Art of Healing in the Scientific Age*, translated by J. Gaiger and N. Walker (Stanford, CA: Stanford University Press, 1996).

Gawande, Atul. *Being Mortal: Medicine and What Matters in the End* (New York: Henry Holt, 2014).

Guignon, Charles. "Editor's Introduction." In Fyodor Dostoevsky, *Dostoevsky's Grand Inquisitor, with Related Chapters for The Brothers Karamazov*, pp. ix–xliii (Indianapolis, IN: Hackett, 1993).

Guignon, Charles. "Heidegger and Kierkegaard on Death: The Existentiell and the Existential." In A. Buben and P. Stokes (eds.), *Kierkegaard and Death*, pp. 184–203 (Bloomington: Indiana University Press, 2011).

Guignon, Charles. *On Being Authentic* (London: Routledge, 2004).

Heidegger, Martin. *The Basic Problems of Phenomenology*, translated by A. Hofstadter (Bloomington: Indiana University Press, 1982).

Heidegger, Martin. *Basic Questions of Philosophy: Selected Problems of Logic*, translated by R. Rojcewicz and A. Schuwer (Bloomington: Indiana University Press, 1994).

Heidegger, Martin. *Being and Time*, translated by J. Macquarrie and E. Robinson (New York: Harper & Row, 1962).

Heidegger, Martin. *The Concept of Time*, translated by W. McNeill (Oxford: Blackwell, 1992).

Heidegger, Martin. *Contributions to Philosophy (From Enowning)*, translated by P. Emad and K. Maly (Bloomington: Indiana University Press, 1999).

Heidegger, Martin. *Discourse on Thinking*, translated by J. Anderson and E. H. Freund (New York: Harper Torchbooks, 1966).

Heidegger, Martin. *Elucidations of Hölderlin's Poetry*, translated by K. Hoeller (Amherst, NY: Humanity Books, 2000).

Heidegger, Martin. *Fundamental Concepts of Metaphysics: World, Finitude, Solitude*, translated by W. McNeill and N. Walker (Bloomington: Indiana University Press, 1995).

Heidegger, Martin. "Meßkirch's Seventh Centennial," translated by T. Sheehan. *Listening* 8.1–3 (1973): 40–57.

Heidegger, Martin. *The Metaphysical Foundations of Logic*, translated by M. Heim (Bloomington: Indiana University Press, 1992).

Heidegger, Martin. *Nietzsche*, vol. 1, translated by D. F. Krell (New York: Harper & Row, 1979).

Heidegger, Martin. "On the Essence of Grounds." translated by W. McNeill. In Martin Heidegger, *Pathmarks*, pp. 136–154 (Cambridge: Cambridge University Press, 1998).

Heidegger, Martin. "On the Essence of Truth," translated by John Sallis. In M. Heidegger, *Basic Writings*, pp. 111–138 (New York: HarperCollins, 1993).

Heidegger, Martin. "The Origin of the Work of Art," translated by A. Hofstadter. In M. Heidegger, *Basic Writings*, pp. 143–203 (New York: HarperCollins, 1993).

Heidegger, Martin. *Plato's Sophist*, translated by R. Rojcewicz and A. Schuwer (Bloomington: Indiana University Press, 1997).

Heidegger, Martin. *The Question Concerning*

Technology and Other Essays, translated by W. Lovitt (New York: Harper Torchbooks, 1977).

Heidegger, Martin. *What Is Called Thinking?* translated by J. Glenn Gray (New York: Harper & Row, 1968).

Heidegger, Martin. "What Is Metaphysics?" translated by J. Sallis. In M. Heidegger, *Basic Writings*, pp. 93–110 (New York: HarperCollins, 1993).

Heikkinen, Riitta-Liisa. "The Experience of Aging and Advanced Old Age: A Ten-Year Follow Up." *Aging & Society* 24 (2004): 567–582.

Hillman, James. *The Force of Character and the Lasting Life* (New York: Ballantine Books, 1999).

Irvine, William. *A Guide to the Good Life: The Ancient Art of Stoic Joy* (Oxford: Oxford University Press, 2009).

Ivanitis, Linda. *Dostoevsky and the Russian People* (Cambridge: Cambridge University Press, 2008).

Jung, Carl G. *Memories, Dreams, Reflections*, translated by R. and C. Winston (London: Collins & Routledge, 1963).

Kaag, John. "How to Live with Dying." *American Scholar*, September 30, 2021.

Kierkegaard, Søren. *The Concept of Anxiety*, translated by W. Lowerie (Princeton, NJ: Princeton University Press, 1944).

Kierkegaard, Søren, *Either/Or*, translated by H. Hong and E. Hong (Princeton, NJ: Princeton University Press, 1987).

Kierkegaard, Søren. *Either/Or*, translated by D. Swenson, L. Swenson, and W. Lowrie. In R. Bretall (ed.), *A Kierkegaard Anthology*, pp. 19–108 (Princeton, NJ: Princeton University Press, 1973).

Kierkegaard, Søren. *Fear and Trembling*, translated by W. Lowrie. In C. Guigon and D. Pereboom (eds.), *Existentialism: Basic Writings*, pp. 26–77 (Indianapolis, IN: Hackett, 2001).

Kierkegaard, Søren. *Journals and Papers*, translated by H. Hong and E. Hong (Bloomington: Indiana University Press, 1975).

Kierkegaard, Søren. *"The Moment" and Late Writings*, translated by H. Hong and E. Hong (Princeton, NJ: Princeton University Press, 1998).

Kierkegaard, Søren. *The Sickness unto Death*, translated by A. Hannay (New York: Penguin Books, 1989).

Kierkegaard, Søren. *Three Discourses on Imagined Occasions*, translated by E. Hong and H. Hong (Princeton, NJ: Princeton University Press, 1993).

Kierkegaard, Søren. *Works of Love*, translated by H. Hong, and E. Hong (Princeton, NJ: Princeton University Press, 1995).

Krauss, Susan and Sneed, Joel. "The Paradox of Well-Being, Identity Processes, and Stereotype Threat: Ageism and its Potential Relationship to the Self in Later Life." In T. Nelson (ed.), *Ageism: Stereotyping and Prejudice against Older Persons*, pp. 247–273 (Cambridge, MA: MIT Press, 2007).

Kruks, Sonia. *Simone de Beauvoir and the Politics of Ambiguity* (Oxford: Oxford University Press, 2012).

Laceulle, Hanne. "Aging and the Ethics of Authenticity." *Gerontologist* 58.5 (2018): 970–978.

Laceulle, Hanne and Baars, Jan. "Self-Realization and Cultural Narratives about Later Life." *Journal of Aging Studies* 31 (2014): 34–44.

Leder, Drew. "What Is It to 'Age Well'? Re-visioning Later Life." In K. Aho (ed.), *Existential Medicine:*

Essays on Health and Illness, pp. 223–234 (London: Rowman & Littlefield, 2018).

Leland, John. *Happiness Is a Choice You Make: Lessons from a Year among the Oldest Old* (New York: Sarah Crichton Books, 2018).

Love, Jeff and Metzger, Jeffrey (eds.). *Nietzsche and Dostoevsky: Philosophy, Morality, Tragedy* (Evanston, IL: Northwestern University Press, 2016).

Marcel, Gabriel. *Being and Having*, translated by K. Farrer (Glasgow: Glasgow University Press, 1949).

Marcel, Gabriel. *Homo Viator: Introduction to a Metaphysics of Hope*, translated by E. Craufurd (Chicago, IL: Henry Regnery Company, 1951).

Marcel, Gabriel. *Mystery of Being: Reflection and Mystery*, vol. 1 (South Bend, IN: Gateway Editions, 1951).

Maritain, Jacques and Maritain, Raïssa. *The Situation of Poetry*, translated by M. Suther (Berkeley, CA: Philosophical Library, 1955).

Marley, Marie. *Come Back Early Today: A Memoir of Love, Alzheimer's and Joy* (Olathe, KS: Joseph Peterson Books, 2011).

Martinsen, Deborah. "Ingratitude and the Underground." *Dostoevsky Studies* (New Series) 17 (2013): 7–12.

Merleau-Ponty, Maurice. *Phenomenology of Perception*, translated by C. Smith (New York: Routledge, 1962).

Merleau-Ponty, Maurice. *The Visible and the Invisible*, translated by A. Lingis (Evanston, IL: Northwestern University Press, 1968).

Moi, Toril. *Simone de Beauvoir: The Making of an Intellectual Woman* (Oxford: Oxford University Press, 2008).

Musset, Shannon. "Ageing and Existentialism: Simone de Beauvoir and the Limits of Freedom." In C. Tandy (ed.), *Death and Anti-Death* (Palo Alto, CA: Ria University Press, 2006).

Nehamas, Alexander. *Nietzsche: Life as Literature* (Cambridge, MA: Harvard University Press, 1985).

Nietzsche, Friedrich. *Beyond Good and Evil*, translated by M. Faber (Oxford: Oxford University Press, 1998).

Nietzsche, Friedrich. *Ecce Homo*, translated by W. Kaufman (New York: Vintage Books, 1989).

Nietzsche, Friedrich. *The Gay Science*, translated by W. Kaufman (New York: Random House, 1974).

Nietzsche, Friedrich. *The Gay Science*, translated by R. Polt. In C. Guignon and D. Pereboom (eds.), *Existentialism: Basic Writings*, pp. 123–171 (Indianapolis, IN: Hackett, 2001).

Nietzsche, Friedrich. *Human, All Too Human: A Book for Free Spirits*, translated by R. J. Hollingdale (Cambridge: Cambridge University Press, 1996).

Nietzsche, Friedrich. *On the Genealogy of Morals*, translated by D. Smith (Oxford: Oxford University Press, 1996).

Nietzsche, Friedrich. "On Truth and Lies in a Nonmoral Sense." In F. Nietzsche, *Philosophy and Truth: Selections from Nietzsche's Notebooks of the Early 1870s*, translated by D. Breazeale (New Jersey: Humanities Library, 1990).

Nietzsche, Friedrich. *Thus Spoke Zarathustra: A Book for All and None*, translated by W. Kaufmann (New York: Penguin Books, 1978).

Nietzsche, Friedrich. *The Twilight of the Idols and The Anti-Christ*, translated by R. J. Hollingdale (New York: Penguin Classics, 1990).

Nietzsche, Friedrich. *The Will to Power*, translated by W. Kaufmann (New York: Vintage Books, 1968).

Nussbaum, Martha and Levmore, Saul. *Aging Thoughtfully: Conversations about Retirement, Romance, Wrinkles, and Regret* (Oxford: Oxford University Press, 2017).

Olds, Sharon. *Odes* (New York: Alfred A. Knopf, 2016).

Olivelle, Patrick. *The Ashrama System: The History and Hermeneutics of a Religious Institution* (Oxford: Oxford University Press, 1993).

Ortega y Gasset, José. *The Revolt of the Masses* (New York: W. W. Norton, 1957).

Ortega y Gasset, José. *Toward a Philosophy of History*, translated by H. Weyl (New York: W. W. Norton, 1941).

Pascal, Blaise. *Pensées*, translated by A. J. Krailsheimer (New York: Penguin Classics, 1966).

Pipher, Mary. *Women Rowing North: Navigating Life's Currents and Flourishing As We Age* (New York: Bloomsbury, 2019).

Ram Dass, Baba. *Still Here: Embracing Aging, Changing, and Dying* (New York: Riverside Books, 2001).

Rilke, Rainer Maria. *The Book of Hours: Love Poems to God*, translated by A. Barrows and J. Macy (New York: Riverhead Books, 2005).

Rilke, Rainer Maria. *The Dark Interval: Letters on Loss, Grief, and Transformation*, translated by U. Baer (New York: Modern Library, 2018).

Rilke, Rainer Maria. *Letters to a Young Poet*, translated by R. Snell (Mineola, NY: Dover Publications, 1962).

Rilke, Rainer Maria. *The Poet's Guide to Life*, translated by U. Baer (New York: Modern Library, 2005).

Rubin, Lillian. *Women of a Certain Age* (New York: Harper & Row, 1979).

Sacks, Oliver. *Gratitude* (New York: Alfred A. Knopf, 2019).

Safranski, Rüdiger. *Nietzsche: A Philosophical Biography* (New York: W. W. Norton, 2002).

Samuel, Lawrence. *Aging in America: A Cultural History* (Philadelphia: University of Pennsylvania Press, 2017).

Sartre, Jean-Paul. *Being and Nothingness*, translated by H. Barnes. In C. Guignon and D. Pereboom (eds.), *Existentialism: Basic Writings*, pp. 309–362 (Indianapolis, IN: Hackett, 2001).

Sartre, Jean-Paul. "The Humanism of Existentialism," translated by B. Frechtman. In C. Guigon and D. Pereboom (eds.), *Existentialism: Basic Writings*, pp. 290–308 (Indianapolis, IN: Hackett, 2001).

Sartre, Jean-Paul. *The War Diaries*, translated by Q. Hoare. In N. Oaklander (ed.), *Existentialist Philosophy: An Introduction*, pp. 379–381 (Upper Saddle River, NJ: Prentice Hall, 1996).

Seneca, Lucius Annaeus. *Letters from a Stoic*, translated by R. Campbell (New York: Penguin Classics, 2004).

Solomon, Robert. "Forward." In R. Emmons and M. McCullough (eds.), *The Psychology of Gratitude*, pp. v–ix (Oxford: Oxford University Press, 2004).

Stambaugh, Joan. "Heidegger, Taoism, and Metaphysics." In G. Parkes (ed.), *Heidegger and Asian Thought*, pp. 79–92 (Honolulu: University of Hawaii Press, 1987).

Stokes, Patrick and Buben, Adam (eds.). *Kierkegaard and Death* (Indianapolis: Indiana University Press, 2011).

Taylor, Charles. *Sources of the Self: The Making of the Modern Identity* (Cambridge, MA: Harvard University Press, 1989).

Tillich, Paul. "Let Us Dare to Have Solitude." *Union Seminary Quarterly Review* 13 (1957): 9–11.

Tolstoy, Leo. *The Death of Ivan Ilych*, translated by A. Maude (New York: Signet Classics, 1960).

Unamuno, Miguel de. *The Tragic Sense of Life*, translated by J. E. Crawford Flitch (New York: Dover Publications, 1954).

Van Leeuwen, Marco. "The Digital Void: E-NNUI and Experience." In B. Pezze and C. Salzani (eds.), *Essays on Boredom and Modernity*, pp. 177–202 (New York: Rodopi Press, 2009).

Wendell, Susan, *The Rejected Body: Feminist Philosophical Reflections on Disability* (London: Routledge, 1996).

Wood, Alex, Joseph, Stephen, Lloyd, Joanna, and Atkins, Samuel. "Gratitude Influences Sleep through the Mechanism of Pre-Sleep Cognitions." *Journal of Psychosomatic Research* 66.1 (2009): 43–48.

Yalom, Irvin. *Existential Psychotherapy* (New York: Basic Books, 1980).

Yalom, Irvin. *Staring at the Sun: Overcoming the Terror of Death* (San Francisco, CA: Jossey-Bass, 2008).

Yalom, Irvin and Yalom, Marilyn, *A Matter of Death and Life* (Stanford, CA: Stanford University Press, 2021).

Young, Julian. *Heidegger's Later Philosophy* (New York: Cambridge University Press, 2000).

Young-Eisendrath, Polly. *The Resilient Spirit: Transforming Suffering into Insight and Renewal* (New York: Addison-Wesley Publishing, 1996).

Index

Index

Index

Index

Index

Index

Index